A Study of the To
Municipal History

Ralph Van Deman Magoffin

Alpha Editions

This edition published in 2024

ISBN : 9789364732000

Design and Setting By
Alpha Editions
www.alphaedis.com
Email - info@alphaedis.com

As per information held with us this book is in Public Domain.
This book is a reproduction of an important historical work. Alpha Editions uses the best technology to reproduce historical work in the same manner it was first published to preserve its original nature. Any marks or number seen are left intentionally to preserve its true form.

Contents

PREFACE. ....- 1 -

CHAPTER I. THE TOPOGRAPHY OF PRÆNESTE. ....- 2 -

CHAPTER II. THE MUNICIPAL GOVERNMENT OF PRÆNESTE. ....- 35 -

NOTES: ....- 62 -

PREFACE.

This study is the first of a series of studies already in progress, in which the author hopes to make some contributions to the history of the towns of the early Latin League, from the topographical and epigraphical points of view.

The author takes this opportunity to thank Dr. Kirby Flower Smith, Head of the Department of Latin, at whose suggestion this study was begun, and under whose supervision and with whose hearty assistance its revision was completed.

He owes his warmest thanks also to Dr. Harry Langford Wilson, Professor of Roman Archæology and Epigraphy, with whom he made many trips to Præneste, and whose help and suggestions were most valuable.

Especially does he wish to testify to the inspiration to thoroughness which came from the teaching and the example of his dearly revered teacher, Professor Basil Lanneau Gildersleeve, Head of the Greek Department, and he acknowledges also with pleasure the benefit from the scholarly methods of Dr. David M. Robinson, and the manifold suggestiveness of the teaching of Dr. Maurice Bloomfield.

The cordial assistance of the author's aunt, Dr. Esther B. Van Deman, Carnegie Fellow in the American School at Rome, both during his stay in Rome and Præneste and since his return to America, has been invaluable, and the privilege afforded him by Professor Dr. Christian Hülsen, of the German Archæological Institute, of consulting the as yet unpublished indices of the sixth volume of the Corpus Inscriptionum Latinarum, is acknowledged with deep gratitude.

The author is deeply grateful for the facilities afforded him in the prosecution of his investigations while he was a resident in Palestrina, and he takes great pleasure in thanking for their courtesies, Cav. Capitano Felice Cicerchia, President of the Archæological Society at Palestrina, his brother, Cav. Emilio Cicerchia, Government Inspector of Antiquities, Professor Pompeo Bernardini, Mayor of the City, and Cav. Francesco Coltellacci, Municipal Secretary.

Finally, he desires to express his cordial appreciation of the kind advice and generous assistance given by Professor John Martin Vincent in connection with the publication of this monograph.

CHAPTER I.
THE TOPOGRAPHY OF PRÆNESTE.

Nearly a half mile out from the rugged Sabine mountains, standing clear from them, and directly in front of the sinuous little valley which the northernmost headstream of the Trerus made for itself, rises a conspicuous and commanding mountain, two thousand three hundred and eighteen feet above the level of the sea, and something more than half that height above the plain below. This limestone mountain, the modern Monte Glicestro, presents on the north a precipitous and unapproachable side to the Sabines, but turns a fairer face to the southern and western plain. From its conical summit the mountain stretches steeply down toward the southwest, dividing almost at once into two rounded slopes, one of which, the Colle di S. Martino, faces nearly west, the other in a direction a little west of south. On this latter slope is situated the modern Palestrina, which is built on the site of the ancient Præneste.

From the summit of the mountain, where the arx or citadel was, it becomes clear at once why Præneste occupied a proud and commanding position among the towns of Latium. The city, clambering up the slope on its terraces, occupied a notably strong position[1], and the citadel was wholly impregnable to assault. Below and south of the city stretched fertile land easy of access to the Prænestines, and sufficiently distant from other strong Latin towns to be safe for regular cultivation. Further, there is to be added to the fortunate situation of Præneste with regard to her own territory and that of her contiguous dependencies, her position at a spot which almost forced upon her a wide territorial influence, for Monte Glicestro faces exactly the wide and deep depression between the Volscian mountains and the Alban Hills, and is at the same time at the head of the Trerus-Liris valley. Thus Præneste at once commanded not only one of the passes back into the highland country of the Æquians, but also the inland routes between Upper and Lower Italy, the roads which made relations possible between the Hernicans, Volscians, Samnites, and Latins. From Præneste the movements of Volscians and Latins, even beyond the Alban Hills and on down in the Pontine district, could be seen, and any hostile demonstrations could be prepared against or forestalled. In short, Præneste held the key to Rome from the south.

Monte Glicestro is of limestone pushed up through the tertiary crust by volcanic forces, but the long ridges which run off to the northwest are of lava, while the shorter and wider ones extending toward the southwest are of tufa. These ridges are from three to seven miles in length. It is shown either by remains of roads and foundations or (in three cases) by the actual presence of modern towns that in antiquity the tip of almost every one of these ridges was occupied by a city. The whole of the tufa and lava plain that stretches out from Præneste toward the Roman Campagna is flat to the eye, and the towns on the tips of the ridges seem so low that their strong military position is overlooked. The tops of these ridges, however, are everywhere more than an hundred feet above the valley and, in addition, their sides are very steep. Thus the towns were practically impregnable except by an attack along the top of the ridge, and as all these ridges run back to the base of the mountain on which Præneste was situated, both these ridges and their towns necessarily were always closely connected with Præneste and dependent upon her.

There is a simple expedient by which a conception of the topography of the country about Præneste can be obtained. Place the left hand, palm down, flat on a table spreading the fingers slightly, then the palm of the right hand on the back of the left with the fingers pointing at right angles to those of the left hand. Imagine that the mountain, on which Præneste lay, rises in the middle of the back of the upper hand, sinks off to the knuckles of both hands, and extends itself in the alternate ridges and valleys which the fingers and the spaces between them represent.

EXTENT OF THE DOMAIN OF PRÆNESTE.

Just as the modern roads and streets in both country and city of ancient territory are taken as the first and best proof of the presence of ancient boundary lines and thoroughfares, just so the territorial jurisdiction of a city in modern Italy, where tradition has been so constant and so strong, is the best proof for the extent of ancient domain.[2] Before trying, therefore, to settle the limits of the domain of Præneste from the provenience of ancient inscriptions, and by deductions from ancient literary sources, and present topographical and archæological arguments, it will be well worth while to trace rapidly the diocesan boundaries which the Roman church gave to Præneste.

The Christian faith had one of its longest and hardest fights at Præneste to overcome the old Roman cult of Fortuna Primigenia. Christianity triumphed completely, and Præneste was so important a place, that it was made one of the six suburban bishoprics,[3] and from that time on there is more or less mention in the Papal records of the diocese of Præneste, or Penestrino as it began to be called.

In the fifth century A.D. there is mention of a gift to a church by Sixtus III, Pope from 432 to 440, of a certain possession in Prænestine territory called Marmorata,[4] which seems best located near the town of Genazzano.

About the year 970 the territory of Præneste was increased in extent by Pope John XIII, who ceded to his sister Stefania a territory that extended back into the mountains to Aqua alta near Subiaco, and as far as the Rivo lato near Genazzano, and to the west and north from the head of the Anio river to the Via Labicana.[5]

A few years later, in 998, because of some troubles, the domain of Præneste was very much diminished. This is of the greatest importance here, because the territory of the diocese in 998 corresponds almost exactly not only to the natural boundaries, but also, as will be shown later, to the ancient boundaries of her domain. The extent of this restricted territory was about five by six miles, and took in Zagarolo, Valmontone, Cave, Rocca di Cave, Capranica, Poli, and Gallicano.[6] These towns form a circle around Præneste and mark very nearly the ancient boundary. The towns of Valmontone, Cave, and Poli, however, although in a great degree dependent upon Præneste, were, I think, just outside her proper territorial domain.

In 1043, when Emilia, a descendant of the Stefania mentioned above, married Stefano di Colonna, Count of Tusculum, Præneste's territory seems to have been enlarged again to its former extent, because in 1080 at Emilia's death, Pope Gregory VII excommunicated the Colonna because they insisted upon retaining the Prænestine territory which had been given as a fief to Stefania, and which upon Emilia's death should have reverted to the Church.[7]

We get a glance again at the probable size of the Prænestine diocese in 1190, from the fact that the fortieth bishop of Præneste was Giovanni Anagnino de' Conti di Segni (1190-1196),[8] and this seems to imply a further extension of the diocese to the southeast down the Trerus (Sacco) valley.

Again, in 1300 after the papal destruction of Palestrina, the government of the city was turned over to Cardinal Ranieri, who was to hold the city and its castle (mons), the mountain and its territory. At this time the diocese comprised the land as far as Artena (Monte Fortino) and and Rocca Priora, one of the towns in the Alban Hills, and to Castrum Novum Tiburtinum, which may well be Corcolle.[9]

The natural limits of the ancient city proper can hardly be mistaken. The city included not only the arx and that portion of the southern slope of the mountain which was walled in, but also a level piece of fertile ground below the city, across the present Via degli Arconi. This piece of flat land has an area about six hundred yards square, the natural boundaries of which are: on the west, the deep bed of the watercourse spanned by the Ponte dei Sardoni; on the east, the cut over which is built the Ponte dell' Ospedalato, and on the south, the depression running parallel to the Via degli Arconi, and containing the modern road from S. Rocco to Cave.

From the natural limits of the town itself we now pass to what would seem to have been the extent of territory dependent upon her. The strongest argument of this discussion is based upon the natural configuration of the land. To the west, the domain of Præneste certainly followed those long fertile ridges accessible only from Præneste. First, and most important, it extended along the very wide ridge known as Le Tende and Le Colonnelle which stretches down toward Gallicano. Some distance above that town it splits, one half, under the name of Colle S. Rocco, running out to the point on which Gallicano is situated, and the other, as the Colle Caipoli, reaching farther out into the Campagna. Along and across this ridge ran several ancient roads.[10] With the combination of fertile ground well situated, in a position farthest away from all hostile attack, and a location not only in plain sight from the citadel of Præneste, but also between Præneste and her closest friend and ally, Tibur, it is certain that in this ridge we have one of the most favored and valuable of Præneste's possessions, and quite as certain that Gallicano, probably the ancient Pedum,[11] was one of the towns which were dependent allies of Præneste. It was along this ridge too that probably the earlier, and certainly the more intimate communication between Præneste and Tibur passed, for of the three possible routes, this was both the nearest and safest.[12]

PLATE I   Præneste, on mountain in background; Gallicano, on top of ridge, in foreground.

The second ridge, called Colle di Pastore as far as the Gallicano cut, and Colle Collafri beyond it, along which for four miles runs the Via Prænestina, undoubtedly belonged to the domain of Præneste.[13] But it was not so important a piece of property as the ridges on either side, for it is much narrower, and it had no town at its end. There was probably always a road out this ridge, as is shown by the presence of the later Via Praenestina, but that there was no town at the end of the ridge is well proved by the fact that Ashby finds no remains there which give evidence of one. Then, too, we have plain enough proof of general unfitness for a town. In the first place the ridge runs off into the junction of two roadless valleys, there is not much fertile land back of where the town site would have been, but above all, however, it is certain that the Via Praenestina was an officially made Roman road, and did not occupy anything more than a previous track of little consequence. This is shown by the absence of tombs of the early necropolis style along this road.

The next ridge must always have been one of the most important, for from above Cavamonte as far as Passerano, at the bottom of the ridge on the side toward Rome, connecting with the highway which was the later Via Latina, ran the main road through Zagarolo, Passerano, Corcolle, on to Tibur and the north.[14] As this was the other of the two great roads which ran to the north without getting out on the Roman Campagna, it is certain that Praeneste considered it in her territory, and probably kept the travel well in hand. With dependent towns at Zagarolo and Passerano, which are several miles distant from each other, there must have been at least one more town between them, to guard the road against attack from Tusculum or Gabii. The fact that the Via Praenestina later cut the Colle del Pero-Colle Seloa just below a point where an ancient road ascends the ridge to a place well adapted for a town, and where there are some remains,[15] seems to prove the supposition, and to locate another of the dependent cities of Praeneste.

That the next ridge, the one on which Zagarolo is situated, was also part of Praeneste's territory, aside from the fact that it has always been part of the diocese of Praeneste, is clearly shown by the topography of the district. The only easy access to Zagarolo is from Palestrina, and although the town itself cannot be seen from the mountain of Praeneste, nevertheless the approach to it along the ridge is clearly visible.

The country south and in front of Praeneste spreads out more like a solid plain for a mile or so before splitting off into the ridges which are so characteristic of the neighborhood. East of the ridge on which Zagarolo stands, and running nearly at right angles to it, is a piece of territory along which runs the present road (the Omata di Palestrina) to the Palestrina railroad station, and which as far as the cross valley at Colle dell'Aquila, is incontestably Praenestine domain.

But the territory which most certainly belonged to Præneste, and which was at once the most valuable and the oldest of her possessions is the wide ridge now known as the Vigne di Loreto, along which runs the road to Marcigliano.[16] Not only does this ridge lie most closely bound to Præneste by nature, but it leads directly toward Velitræ, her most advantageous ally. Tibur was perhaps always Præneste's closest and most loyal ally, but the alliance with her had not the same opportunity for mutual advantage as one with Velitræ, because each of these towns commanded the territory the other wished to know most about, and both together could draw across the upper Trerus valley a tight line which was of the utmost importance from a strategic point of view. These two facts would in themselves be a satisfactory proof that this ridge was Præneste's first expansion and most important acquisition, but there is proof other than topographical and argumentative.

At the head of this ridge in la Colombella, along the road leading to Marcigliano from the little church of S. Rocco, have been found three strata of tombs. The line of graves in the lowest stratum, the date of which is not later than the fifth or sixth century B.C., points exactly along the ancient road, now the Via della Marcigliana or di Loreto.[17]

The natural limit of Prænestine domain to the south has now been reached, and that it is actually the natural limit is shown by the accompanying illustration.

Through the Valle di Pepe or Fosso dell' Ospedalato (see Plate II), which is wide as well as deep, runs the uppermost feeder of the Trerus river. One sees at a glance that the whole slope of the mountain from arx to base is continued by a natural depression which would make an ideal boundary for Prænestine territory. Nor is the topographical proof all. No inscriptions of consequence, and no architectural remains of the pre-imperial period have been found across this valley. The road along the top of the ridge beyond it is an ancient one, and ran to Valmontone as it does today, and was undoubtedly often used between Præneste and the towns on the Volscians. The ridge, however, was exposed to sudden attack from too many directions to be of practical value to Præneste. Valmontone, which lay out beyond the end of this ridge, commanded it, and Valmontone was not a dependency of Præneste, as is shown by an inscription which mentions the adlectio of a citizen there into the senate (decuriones) of Præneste.[18]

There are still two other places which as we have seen were included at different times in the papal diocese of Præneste,[19] namely, Capranica and Cave.[20] Inscriptional evidence is not forthcoming in either place sufficient to warrant any certainty in the matter of correspondence of local names to those in Præneste. Of the two, Capranica had much more need of dependence on Præneste than Cave. It was down through the little valley back of Præneste, at the head of which Capranica lay, that her later aqueducts came. The outlet from Capranica back over the mountains was very difficult, and the only tillable soil within reach of that town lay to the north of Præneste on the ridge running toward Gallicano, and on a smaller ridge which curved around toward Tibur and lay still closer to the mountains. In short, Capranica, which never attained importance enough to be of any consequence, appears to have been always dependent upon Præneste.

But as for Cave, that is another question. Her friends were to the east, and there was easy access into the mountains to Sublaqueum (Subiaco) and beyond, through the splendid passes via either of the modern towns, Genazzano or Olevano.

Plate II. Præneste, Monte Ginestro with citadel, as seen from Valle di Pepe.

It is quite evident that Cave was never a large town, and it seems most probable that she realized that an amicable understanding with Præneste was discreet. This is rendered almost certain by the proof of a continuance of business relations between the two places. The greater number of the big tombs of the sixth and fifth centuries B.C. are of a peperino from Cave,[21] and a good deal of the tufa used in wall construction in Præneste is from the quarries near Cave, as Fernique saw.[22]

Rocca di Cave, on a hill top behind Cave, is too insignificant a location to have been the cause of the lower town, which at the best does not itself occupy a very advantageous position in any way, except that it is in the line of a trade route from lower Italy. It might be maintained with some reason that Cave was a settlement of dissatisfied merchants from Præneste, who had gone out and established themselves on the main road for the purpose of anticipating the trade, but there is much against such an argument.

It has been shown that there were peaceable relations between Præneste and Cave in the fifth and sixth centuries B.C., but that the two towns were on terms of equality is impossible, and that Cave was a dependency of Præneste, and in her domain, is most unlikely both topographically and epigraphically. And more than this, just as an ancient feud can be proved between Præneste and Rome from the slurs on Præneste which one finds in literature from Plautus down,[23] if no other proofs were to be had,[24] just so there is a very ancient grudge between Præneste and Cave, which has been perpetuated and is very noticeable even at the present day.[25]

The topography of Præneste as to the site of the city proper, and as to its territorial domain is then, about as follows.

In very early times, probably as early as the ninth or tenth century B.C., Præneste was a town on the southern slope of Monte Glicestro,[26] with an arx on the summit. As the town grew, it spread first to the level ground directly below, and out along the ridge west of the Valle di Pepe toward Marcigliano, because it was territory not only fertile and easily defended, being directly under the very eyes of the citizens, but also because it stretched out toward Velitræ, an old and trusted ally.[27]

Her next expansion was in the direction of Tibur, along the trade route which followed the Sabine side of the Liris-Trerus valley, and this expansion gave her a most fertile piece of territory. To insure this against incursions from the pass which led back into the mountains, it seems certain that Præneste secured or perhaps colonized Capranica.

The last Prænestine expansion in territory had a motive beyond the acquisition of land, for it was also important from a strategical point of view. It will be remembered that the second great trade route which came into the Roman plain ran past Zagarolo, Passerano, and Corcolle.[28] This road runs along a valley just below ridges which radiate from the mountain on which Præneste is situated, and thus bordered the land which was by nature territory dependent upon Præneste.[29] So this final extension of her domain was to command this important road. With the carrying out of this project all the ridges mentioned above came gradually into the possession of Praneste, as natural, expedient, and unquestioned domain, and on the ends of those ridges which were defensible, dependent towns grew up. There was also a town at Cavamonte above the Maremmana road, probably a village out on the Colle dell'Oro, and undoubtedly one at Marcigliano, or in that vicinity.

We have already seen that across a valley and a stream of some consequence there is a ridge not at all connected with the mountain on which Præneste was situated, but belonging rather to Valmontone, which was better suited for neutral ground or to act as a buffer to the southeast.

We turn to mention this ridge again as territory topographically outside Præneste's domain, in order to say more forcibly that one must cross still another valley and stream before reaching the territory of Cave, and so Cave, although dependent upon Præneste, by reason of its size and interests, was not a dependent city of Præneste, nor was it a part of her domain.[30]

In short, to describe Præneste, that famous town of Latium, and her domain in a true if homely way, she was an ancient and proud city whose territory was a commanding mountain and a number of ridges running out from it, which spread out like a fan all the way from the Fosso dell'Ospedalato (the depression shown in plate II) to the Sabine mountains on the north.

THE CITY, ITS WALLS AND GATES.

The general supposition has been that the earliest inhabitants of Præneste lived only in the citadel on top of the hill. This theory is supported by the fact that there is room enough, and, as will be shown below, there was in early times plenty of water there; nevertheless it is certain that this was not the whole of the site of the early city.

The earliest inhabitants of Præneste needed first of all, safety, then a place for pasturage, and withal, to be as close to the fertile land at the foot of the mountain as possible. The first thing the inhabitants of the new city did was to build a wall. There is still a little of this oldest wall in the circuit about the citadel, and it was built at exactly the same time as the lower part of the double walls that extend down the southern slope of the mountain on each side of the upper part of the modern town. It happens that by following the edges of the slope of this southern face of the mountain down to a certain point, one realizes that even without a wall the place would be practically impregnable. Add to this the fact that all the stones necessary for a wall were obtained during the scarping of the arx on the side toward the Sabines,[31] and needed only to be rolled down, not up, to their places in the wall, which made the task a very easy one comparatively. Now if a place can be found which is naturally a suitable place for a lower cross wall, we shall have what an ancient site demanded; first, safety, because the site now proposed is just as impregnable as the citadel itself, and still very high above the plain below; second, pasturage, for on the slope between the lower town and the arx is the necessary space which the arx itself hardly supplies; and third, a more reasonable nearness to the fertile land below. All the conditions necessary are fulfilled by a cross wall in Præneste, which up to this time has remained mostly unknown, often neglected or wrongly described, and wholly misunderstood. As we shall see, however, this very wall was the lower boundary of the earliest Præneste. The establishment of this important fact will remove one of the many stumbling blocks over which earlier writers on Præneste have fallen.

It has been said above that the lowest part of the wall of the arx, and the two walls from it down the mountain were built at the same time. The accompanying plate (III) shows very plainly the course of the western wall as it comes down the hill lining the edge of the slope where it breaks off most sharply. Porta San Francesco, the modern gate, is above the second tree from the right in the illustration, just where the wall seems to turn suddenly. There is no trace of ancient wall after the gate is passed. The white wall, as one proceeds from the gate to the right, is the modern wall of the Franciscan monastery. All the writers on Præneste say that the ancient wall came on around the town where the lower wall of the monastery now is, and followed the western limit of the present town as far as the Porta San Martino.

Returning now to plate II we observe a thin white line of wall which joins a black line running off at an angle to our left. This is also a piece of the earliest cyclopean wall, and it is built just at the eastern edge of the hill where it falls off very sharply.

Now if one follows the Via di San Francesco in from the gate of that name (see plate III again) and then continues down a narrow street east of the monastery as far as the open space in front of the church of Santa Maria del Carmine, he will see that on his left above him the slope of the mountain was not only precipitous by nature but that also it has been rendered entirely unassailable by scarping.[32] From the lower end of this steep escarpment there is a cyclopean wall, of the same date as the upper side walls of the town, and the wall of the arx, which runs entirely across the city to within a few yards of the wall on the east, and to a point just below a portella, where the upper cyclopean wall makes a slight change in direction. The presence of the gate and the change of direction in the wall mean a corner in the wall.

PLATE III. The western cyclopean wall of Præneste, and the depression which divides Monte Glicestro.

It is strange indeed that this wall has not been recognized for what it really is. A bit of it shows above the steps where the Via dello Spregato leaves the Via del Borgo. Fernique shows this much in his map, but by a curious oversight names it opus incertum.[33] More than two irregular courses are to be seen here, and fifteen feet in from the street, forming the back wall of cellars and pig pens, the cyclopean wall, in places to a height of fifteen feet or more, can be followed to within a few yards of the open space in front of Santa Maria del Carmine. And on the other side toward the east the same wall begins again, after being broken by the Via dello Spregato, and forms the foundations and side walls of the houses on the south side of that street, and at the extreme east end is easily found as the back wall of a blacksmith's shop at the top of the Via della Fontana, and can be identified as cyclopean by a little cleaning of the wall.

The circuit of the earliest cyclopean wall and natural ramparts of the contemporaneous citadel and town of Præneste was as follows: An arc of cyclopean wall below the cap of the hill which swung round from the precipitous cliff on the west to that on the east, the whole of the side of the arx toward the mountains being so steep that no wall was necessary; then a second loop of cyclopean wall from the arx down the steep western edge of the southern slope of the mountain as far as the present Porta San Francesco. From this point natural cliffs reinforced at the upper end by a short connecting wall bring us to the beginning of the wall which runs across the town back of the Via del Borgo from Santa Maria del Carmine to within a short distance of the east wall of the city, separated from it in fact only by the Via della Fontana, which runs up just inside the wall. There it joins the cyclopean wall which comes down from the citadel on the east side of the town.

The reasons why this is the oldest circuit of the city's walls are the following: first, all this stretch of wall is the oldest and was built at the same time; second, topography has marked out most clearly that the territory inclosed by these walls, here and only here, fulfills the two indispensable requisites of the ancient town, namely space and defensibility; third, below the gate San Francesco all the way round the city as far as Porta del Sole, neither in the wall nor in the buildings, nor in the valley below, is there any trace of cyclopean wall stones;[34] fourth, at the point where the cross wall and the long wall must have met at the east, the wall makes a change in direction, and there is an ancient postern gate just above the jog in the wall; and last, the cyclopean wall from this junction on down to near the Porta del Sole is later than that of the circuit just described.[35]

The city was extended within a century perhaps, and the new line of the city wall was continued on the east in cyclopean style as far as the present Porta del Sole, where it turned to the west and continued until the hill itself offered enough height so that escarpment of the natural cliff would serve in place of the wall. Then it turned up the hill between the present Via San Biagio and Via del Carmine back of Santa Maria del Carmine. The proof for this expansion is clear. The continuation of the cyclopean wall can be seen now as far as the Porta del Sole,[36] and the line of the wall which turns to the west is positively known from the cippi of the ancient pomerium, which were found in 1824 along the present Via degli Arconi.[37] The ancient gate, now closed, in the opus quadratum wall under the Cardinal's garden, is in direct line with the ancient pavement of the road which comes up to the city from the south,[38] and the continuation of that road, which seems to have been everywhere too steep for wagons, is the Via del Carmine. There had always been another road outside the wall which went up a less steep grade, and came round the angle of the wall at what is now the Porta S. Martino, where it entered a gate that opened out of the present Corso toward the west. When at a later time, probably in the middle ages, the city was built out to its present boundary on the west, the wagon road was simply arched over, and this arch is now the gate San Martino.[39]

It will be necessary to speak further of the cyclopean wall on the east side of the city from the Porta del Sole to the Portella, for it has always been supposed that this part of the wall was exactly like the rest, and dated from the same period. But a careful examination shows that the stones in this lower portion are laid more regularly than those in the wall above the Portella, that they are more flatly faced on the outside, and that here and there a little mortar is used. Above all, however, there is in the wall on one of the stones under the house no. 24, Via della Fontana an inscription,[40] which Richter, Dressel, and Dessau all think was there when the stone was put in the wall, and incline to allow no very remote date for the building of the wall at that point. To me, after a comparative study of this wall and the one at Norba, the two seem to date from very nearly the same time, and no one now dares attribute great antiquity to the walls of Norba. But the rest of the cyclopean wall of Præneste is very ancient, certainly a century, perhaps two or three centuries, older than the part from the Portella down.

There remains still to be discussed the lower wall of the city on the south, and a restraining terrace wall along part of the present Corso Pierluigi. The stretch of city wall from the Porta del Sole clear across the south front to the Porta di S. Martino is of opus quadratum, with the exception of a stretch of opus incertum[41] below and east of the Barberini gardens, and a small space where the city sewage has destroyed all vestige of a wall. The restraining wall just mentioned is also of opus quadratum and is to be found along the south side of the Corso, but can be seen only from the winecellars on the terrace below that street. These walls of opus quadratum were built with a purpose, to be sure, but their entire meaning has not been understood.[42]

The upper wall, the one along the Corso, can not be traced farther than the Piazza Garibaldi, in front of the Cathedral. It has been a mistake to consider this a high wall. It was built simply to level up with the Corso terrace, partly to give more space on the terrace, partly to make room for a road which ran across the city here between two gates no longer in existence. But more especially was it built to be the lower support for a gigantic water reservoir which extends under nearly the whole width of this terrace from about Corso Pierluigi No. 88 almost to the Cathedral.[43] The four sides of this great reservoir are also of opus quadratum laid header and stretcher.

The lower wall, the real town wall, is a wall only in appearance, for it has but one thickness of blocks, set header and stretcher in a mass of solid concrete.[44] This wall makes very clear the impregnability of even the lower part of Præneste, for the wall not only occupies a good position, but is really a double line of defense. There are here two walls, one above the other, the upper one nineteen feet back of the lower, thus leaving a terrace of that width.[45] At the east, instead of the lower solid wall of opus quadratum, there is a series of fine tufa arches built to serve as a substructure for something. It is to be remembered again that between the arches on the east and the solid wall on the west is a stretch of 200 feet of opus incertum, and a space where there is no wall at all. This lower wall of Præneste occupies the same line as the ancient wall and escarpment, but the most of what survives was restored in Sulla's time. The opus quadratum is exactly the same style as that in the Tabularium in Rome.

Now, no one could see the width of the terrace above the lower wall, without thinking that so great a width was unnecessary unless it was to give room for a road.[46] The difficulty has been, however, that the line of arches at the east, not being in alignment with the lower wall on the west, has not been connected with it hitherto, and so a correct understanding of their relation has been impossible.

Before adducing evidence to show the location of the main and triumphal entrance to Præneste, we shall turn to the town above for a moment to see whether it is, a priori, reasonable to suppose that there was an entrance to the city here in the center of its front wall. If roads came up a grade from the east and west, they would join at a point where now there is no wall at all. This break is in the center of the south wall, just above the forum which was laid out in Sulla's time on the level spot immediately below the town. Most worthy of note, however, is that this opening is straight below the main buildings of the ancient town, the basilica, which is now the cathedral, and the temple of Fortuna. But further, a fact which has never been noticed nor accounted for, this opening is also in front of the modern square, the piazza Garibaldi, which is in front of the buildings just mentioned but below them on the next terrace, yet there is no entrance to this terrace shown.[47] It is well known that the open space south of the temple, beside the basilica, has an ancient pavement some ten feet below the present level of the modern piazza Savoia.[48] Proof given below in connection with the large tufa base which is on the level of the lower terrace will show that the piazza Garibaldi was an open space in ancient times and a part of the ancient forum. Again, the solarium, which is on the south face of the basilica,[49] was put up there that it might be seen, and as it faces the south, the piazza Garibaldi, and this open space in the wall under discussion, what is more likely than that there was not only an open square below the basilica, but also the main approach to the city?

But now for the proof. In 1756 ancient paving stones were still in situ[50] above the row of arches on the Via degli Arconi, and even yet the ascent is plain enough to the eye. The ground slopes up rather moderately along the Via degli Arconi toward the east, and nearly below the southeast corner of the ancient wall turned up to the west on these arches, approaching the entrance in the middle of the south wall of the city.[51] But these arches and the road on them do not align exactly with the terrace on the west. Nor should they do so. The arches are older than the present opus quadratum wall, and the road swung round and up to align with the road below and the old wall or escarpment of the city above. Then when the whole town, its gates, its walls, and its temple, were enlarged and repaired by Sulla, the upper wall was perfectly aligned, a lower wall built on the west leaving a terrace for a road, and the arches were left to uphold the road on the east. Although the arches were not exactly in line, the road could well have been so, for the terrace here was wider and ran back to the upper wall.[52] The evidence is also positive enough that there was an ascent to the terrace on the west, the one below the Barberini gardens, which corresponds to the ascent on the arches. This terrace now is level, and at its west end is some twenty feet above the garden below. But the wall shows very plainly that it had sloped off toward the west, and the slope is most clearly to be seen, where a very obtuse angle of newer and different tufa has been laid to build up the wall to a level.[53] It is to be noticed too that this terrace is the same height as the top of the ascent above the arches. We have then actual proofs for roads leading up from east and west toward the center of the wall on the south side of the city, and every reason that an entrance here was practicable, credible, and necessary.

But there is one thing more necessary to make probabilities tally wholly with the facts. If there was a grand entrance to the city, below the basilica, the temple, and the main open square, which faced out over the great forum below, there must have been a monumental gate in the wall. As a matter of fact there was such a gate, and I believe it was called the PORTA TRIUMPHALIS. An inscription of the age of the Antonines mentions "seminaria a Porta Triumphale," and this passing reference to a gate with a name which in itself implies a gate of consequence, so well known that a building placed near it at once had its location fixed, gives the rest of the proof necessary to establish a central entrance to the city in front, through a PORTA TRIUMPHALIS.[54]

Before the time of Sulla there had been a gate in the south wall of the city, approached by one road, which ascended from the east on the arches facing the present Via degli Arconi. After entering the city one went straight up a grade not very steep to the basilica, and to the open square or ancient forum which was the space now occupied by the two modern piazzas, the Garibaldi and the Savoia, and on still farther to the temple. When Sulla rebuilt the city, and laid out a forum on the level space directly south of and below the town, he made another road from the west to correspond to the old ascent from the east, and brought them together at the old central gate, which he enlarged to the PORTA TRIUMPHALIS. In the open square in front of the basilica had stood the statue of some famous man[55] on a platform of squared stone 16 x 17-1/2 feet in measurement. Around this base the Sullan improvements put a restraining wall of opus quadratum.[56] The open square was in front of the basilica and to its left below the temple. There was but one way to the terrace above the temple from the ancient forum. This was a steep road to the right, up the present Via delle Scalette. Another road ran to the left back of the basilica, but ended either in front of the western cave connected with the temple, or at the entrance into the precinct of the temple.

THE GATES.

Strabo, in a well known passage,[57] speaks of Tibur and Præneste as two of the most famous and best fortified of the towns of Latium, and tells why Præneste is the more impregnable, but we have no mention of its gates in literature, except incidentally in Plutarch,[58] who says that when Marius was flying before Sulla's forces and had reached Præneste, he found the gates closed, and had to be drawn up the wall by a rope. The most ancient reference we have to a definite gate is to the Porta Triumphalis, in the inscription just mentioned, and this is the only gate of Præneste mentioned by name in classic times.

In 1353 A.D. we have two gates mentioned. The Roman tribune Cola di Rienzo (Niccola di Lorenzo) brought his forces out to attack Stefaniello Colonna in Præneste. It was not until Rienzo moved his camp across from the west to the east side of the plain below the town that he saw how the citizens were obtaining supplies. The two gates S. Cesareo and S. Francesco[59] were both being utilized to bring in supplies from the mountains back of the city, and the stock was driven to and from pasture through these gates. These gates were both ancient, as will be shown below. Again in 1448 when Stefano Colonna rebuilt some walls after the awful destruction of the city by Cardinal Vitelleschi, he opened three gates, S. Cesareo, del Murozzo, and del Truglio.[60] In 1642[61] two more gates were opened by Prince Taddeo Barberini, the Porta del Sole, and the Porta delle Monache, the former at the southeast corner of the town, the latter in the east wall at the point where the new wall round the monastery della Madonna degl'Angeli struck the old city wall, just above the present street where it turns from the Via di Porta del Sole into the Corso Pierluigi. This Porta del Sole[62] was the principal gate of the town at this time, or perhaps the one most easily defended, for in 1656, during the plague in Rome, all the other gates were walled up, and this one alone left open.[63]

The present gates of the city are: one, at the southeast corner, the Porta del Sole; two, near the southwest corner, where the wall turns up toward S. Martino, a gate now closed;[64] three, Porta S. Martino, at the southwest corner of the town; on the west side of the city, none at all; four, Porta S. Francesco at the northwest corner of the city proper; five, a gate in the arx wall, now closed,[65] beside the mediæval gate, which is just at the head of the depression shown in plate III, the lowest point in the wall of the citadel; on the east, Porta S. Cesareo, some distance above the town, six; seven, Porta dei Cappuccini, which is on the same terrace as Porta S. Francesco;

eight, Portella, the eastern outlet of the Via della Portella; nine, a postern just below the Portella, and not now in use;[66] ten, Porta delle Monache or Santa Maria, in front of the church of that name. The most ancient of these, and the ones which were in the earliest circle of the cyclopean wall, are five in number: Porta S. Francesco,[67] the gate into the arx, Porta S. Cesareo,[68] Porta dei Cappuccini, and the postern at the corner where the early cyclopean cross wall struck the main wall.

The second wall of the city, which was rather an enlargement of the first, was cyclopean on the east as far as the present Porta del Sole, and either scarped cliff or opus quadratum round to Porta S. Martino, and up to Porta S. Francesco.[69] At the east end of the modern Corso, there was a gate, made of opus quadratum,[70] as is shown not only by the fact that this is the main street of the city, and on the terrace level of the basilica, but also because the mediæval wall round the monastery of the Madonna degl'Angeli, the grounds of the present church of Santa Maria, did not run straight to the cyclopean wall, but turned down to join it near the gate which it helps to prove. Next, there was a gate, but in all probability only a postern, near the Porta del Sole where the cyclopean wall stops, where now there is a narrow street which runs up to the piazza Garibaldi. On the south there was the gate which at some time was given the name Porta Triumphalis. It was at the place where now there is no wall at all.[71] At the southwest we find the next gate, the one which is now closed.[72] The last one of the ancient gates in this second circle of the city wall was one just inside the modern Porta S. Martino, which opened west at the end of the Corso. All the rest of the gates are mediæval.

A few words about the roads leading to the several gates of Præneste will help further to settle the antiquity of these gates.[73] The oldest road was certainly the trade route which came up the north side of the Liris valley below the hill on which Præneste was situated, and which followed about the line of the Via Prænestina as shown by Ashby in his map.[74] Two branch roads from this main track ran up to the town, one at the west, the other at the east, both in the same line as the modern roads. These roads were bound for the city gates as a matter of course and the land slopes least sharply where these roads were and still are. Another important road was outside the city wall, from one gate to the other, and took the slope on the south side of the city where the Via degli Arconi now runs.[75]

As far as excavations have proved up to this time, the oldest road out of Præneste is that which is now the Via della Marcigliana, along which were found the very early tombs. It is to be noted that these tombs begin beyond the church of S. Rocco, which is a long distance below the town. This distance however makes it certain that between S. Rocco and the city, excavation will bring to light other and yet older tombs along the road which leads up toward "l'antica porta S. Martino chiusa," and also in all probability rows of graves will be found along the present road to Cave. But the tombs give us the direction at least of the old road.[76]

There is yet another old road which was lately discovered. It is about three hundred yards below the city and near the road that cuts through from Porta del Sole to the church of Madonna dell'Aquila.[77] This road is made of polygonal stones of the limestone of the mountain, and hence is older than any of the lava roads. It runs nearly parallel with the Via degli Arconi, and takes a direction which would strike the Via Præenestina where it crosses the Via Præenestina Nuova which runs past Zagarolo. That is, the most ancient piece of road we have leads up to the southeast corner of the town, but the oldest tombs point to a road the direction of which was toward the southwest corner. However, all the roads lead toward the southeast corner, where the old grade began that went up above the arches, mentioned above, to a middle gate of the city.

The gate S. Francesco also is proved to be ancient because of the old road that led from it. This road is identified by a deposit of ex voto terracottas which were found at the edge of the road in a hole hollowed out in the rocks.[78]

The two roads which were traveled the most were the ones that led toward Rome. This is shown by the tombs on both sides of them,[79] and by the discovery of a deposit of a great quantity of ex voto terracottas in the angle between the two.[80]

THE WATER SUPPLY OF PRÆNESTE.

In very early times there was a spring near the top of Monte Glicestro. This is shown by a glance back at plate III, which indicates the depression or cut in the hill, which from its shape and depth is clearly not altogether natural and attributable to the effects of rain, but is certainly the effect of a spring, the further and positive proof of the existence of which is shown by the unnecessarily low dip made by the wall of the citadel purposely to inclose the head of this depression. There are besides no water reservoirs inside the wall of the arx. This supply of water, however, failed, and it must have failed rather early in the city's history, perhaps at about the time the lower part of the city was walled in, for the great reservoir on the Corso terrace seems to be contemporary with this second wall.

But at all times Præneste was dependent upon reservoirs for a sure and lasting supply of water. The mountain and the town were famous because of the number of water reservoirs there.[81] A great many of these reservoirs were dependent upon catchings from the rain,[82] but before a war, or when the rainfall was scant, they were filled undoubtedly from springs outside the city. In later times they were connected with the aqueducts which came to the city from beyond Capranica.

It is easy to account now for the number of gates on the east side of the city. True, this side of the wall lay away from the Campagna, and egress from gates on this side could not be seen by an enemy unless he moved clear across the front of the city.[83] But the real reason for the presence of so many gates is that the best and most copious springs were on this side of the city, as well as the course of the little headstream of the Trerus. The best concealed egress was from the Porta Cesareo, from which a road led round back of the mountain to a fine spring, which was high enough above the valley to be quite safe.

There are no references in literature to aqueducts which brought water to Præneste. Were we left to this evidence alone, we should conclude that Præneste had depended upon reservoirs for water. But in inscriptions we have mention of baths,[84] the existence of which implies aqueducts, and there is the specus of an aqueduct to be seen outside the Porta S. Francesco.[85] This ran across to the Colle S. Martino to supply a large brick reservoir of imperial date.[86] There were aqueducts still in 1437, for Cardinal Vitelleschi captured Palestrina by cutting off its water supply.[87] This shows that the water came from outside the city, and through aqueducts which probably dated back to Roman times,[88] and also that the reservoirs were at this time no longer used. In 1581 the city undertook to restore the old aqueduct which brought water from back of Capranica, but no description was left of its exact course or ancient construction.[89] While these repairs were in progress, Francesco Cecconi leased to the city his property called Terreni, where there were thirty fine springs of clear water not far from the city walls. Again in 1776 the springs called delle cannuccete sent in dirty water to the city, so citizens were appointed to remedy matters. They added a new spring to those already in use and this water came to the city through an aqueduct.[90]

The remains of four great reservoirs, all of brick construction, are plainly enough to be seen at Palestrina, and as far as situation and size are concerned, are well enough described in other places.[91] But in the case of these reservoirs, as in that of all the other remains of ancient construction at Præneste, the writers on the history of the town have made great mistakes, because all of them have been predisposed to the pleasant task of making all the ruins fit some restoration or other of the temple of Fortuna, although, as a matter of fact, none of the reservoirs have any connection whatever with the temple.[92] The fine brick reservoir of the time of Tiberius,[93] which is at the junction of the Via degli Arconi and the road from the Porta S. Martino, was not built to supply fountains or baths in the forum below, but was simply a great supply reservoir for the citizens who lived in particular about the lower forum, and the water from this reservoir was carried away by hand, as is shown by the two openings like well heads in the top of each compartment of the reservoir, and by the steps which gave entrance to it on the east. The reservoir above this in the Barberini gardens is of a date a half century later.[94] It is of the same brick work as the great fountain which stands, now debased to a grist mill, across the Via degli Arconi about half way between S. Lucia and Porta del Sole. The upper reservoir undoubtedly supplied this fountain, and other public buildings in the forum below. There is another large brick reservoir below the present ground level in the angle between the Via degli Arconi and the Cave road below the Porta del Sole, but it is too low ever to have served for public use. It was in connection with some private bath. The fourth huge reservoir, the one on Colle S. Martino, has already been mentioned.

But the most ancient of all the reservoirs is one which is not mentioned anywhere. It dates from the time when the Corso terrace was made, and is of opus quadratum like the best of the wall below the city, and the wall on the lower side of the terrace.[95] This reservoir, like the one in the Barberini garden, served the double purpose of a storage for water, and of a foundation for the terrace, which, being thus widened, offered more space for street and buildings above. It lies west of the basilica, but has no connection with the temple. From its position it seems rather to have been one of the secret public water supplies.[96]

Præneste had in early times only one spring within the city walls, just inside the gate leading into the arx. There were other springs on the mountain to the east and northeast, but too far away to be included within the walls. Because of their height above the valley, they were to a certain extent available even in times of warfare and siege. As the upper spring dried up early, and the others were a little precarious, an elaborate system of reservoirs was developed, a plan which the natural terraces of the mountain slope invited, and a plan which gave more space to the town itself with the work of leveling necessary for the reservoirs. These reservoirs were all public property. They were at first dependent upon collection from rains or from spring water carried in from outside the city walls. Later, however, aqueducts were made and connected with the reservoirs.

With the expansion of the town to the plain below, this system gave great opportunity for the development of baths, fountains, and waterworks,[97] for Præneste wished to vie with Tibur and Rome, where the Anio river and the many aqueducts had made possible great things for public use and municipal adornment.

THE TEMPLE OF FORTUNA PRIMIGENIA.

Nusquam se fortunatiorem quam Præneste vidisse Fortunam.[98] In this way Cicero reports a popular saying which makes clear the fame of the goddess Fortuna Primigenia and her temple at Præneste.[99]

The excavations at Præneste in the eighteenth century brought the city again into prominence, and from that time to the present, Præneste has offered much material for archæologists and historians.

But the temple of Fortuna has constituted the principal interest and engaged the particular attention of everyone who has worked upon the history of the town, because the early enthusiastic view was that the temple occupied the whole slope of the mountain,[100] and that the present city was built on the terraces and in the ruins of the temple. Every successive study, however, of the city from a topographical point of view has lessened more and more the estimated size of the temple, until now all that can be maintained successfully is that there are two separate temples built at different times, the later and larger one occupying a position two terraces higher than the older and more important temple below.

The lower temple with its precinct, along the north side of which extends a wall and the ruins of a so-called cryptoporticus which connected two caves hollowed out in the rock, is not so very large a sanctuary, but it occupies a very good position above and behind the ancient forum and basilica on a terrace cut back into the solid rock of the mountain. The temple precinct is a courtyard which extends along the terrace and occupies its whole width from the older cave on the west to the newer one at the east. In front of the latter cave is built the temple itself, which faces west along the terrace, but extends its southern facade to the edge of the ancient forum which it overlooks. This temple is older than the time of Sulla, and occupies the site of an earlier temple.

Two terraces higher, on the Cortina terrace, stretch out the ruins of a huge construction in opus incertum. This building had at least two stories of colonnade facing the south, and at the north side of the terrace a series of arches above which in the center rose a round temple which was approached by a semicircular flight of steps.[101] This building, belonging to the time of Sulla, presented a very imposing appearance from the forum below the town. It has no connection with the lower temple unless perhaps by underground passages.

Although this new temple and complex of buildings was much larger and costlier than the temple below, it was so little able to compete with the fame of the ancient shrine, that until mediæval times there is not a mention of it anywhere by name or by suggestion, unless perhaps in one inscription mentioned below. The splendid publication of Delbrueck[102] with maps and plans and bibliography of the lower temple and the work which has been done on it, makes unnecessary any remarks except on some few points which have escaped him.

The tradition was that a certain Numerius Suffustius of Præneste was warned in dreams to cut into the rocks at a certain place, and this he did before his mocking fellow citizens, when to the bewilderment of them all pieces of wood inscribed with letters of the earliest style leaped from the rock. The place where this phenomenon occurred was thus proved divine, the cult of Fortuna Primigenia was established beyond peradventure, and her oracular replies to those who sought her shrine were transmitted by means of these lettered blocks.[103] This story accounts for a cave in which the lots (sortes) were to be consulted.

But there are two caves. The reason why there are two has never been shown, nor does Delbrueck have proof enough to settle which is the older cave.[104]

The cave to the west is made by Delbrueck the shrine of Iuppiter puer, and the temple with its cave at the east, the ædes Fortunæ. This he does on the authority of his understanding of the passage from Cicero which gives nearly all the written information we have on the subject of the temple.[105] Delbrueck bases his entire argument on this passage and two other references to a building called ædes.[106] Now it was Fortuna who was worshipped at Præneste, and not Jupiter. Although there is an intimate connection between Jupiter and Fortuna at Præneste, because she was thought of at different times as now the mother and now the daughter of Jupiter, still the weight of evidence will not allow any such importance to be attached to Iuppiter puer as Delbrueck wishes.[107]

The two caves were not made at the same time. This is proved by the fact that the basilica[108] is below and between them. Had there been two caves at the earliest time, with a common precinct as a connection between them, as there was later, there would have been power enough in the priesthood to keep the basilica from occupying the front of the place which would have been the natural spot for a temple or for the imposing facade of a portico. The western cave is the earlier, but it is the earlier not because it was a shrine of Iuppiter puer, but because the ancient road which came through the forum turned up to it, because it is the least symmetrical of the two caves, and because the temple faced it, and did not face the forum.

The various plans of the temple[109] have usually assumed like buildings in front of each cave, and a building, corresponding to the basilica, between them and forming an integral part of the plan. But the basilica does not quite align with the temple, and the road back of the basilica precludes any such idea, not to mention the fact that no building the size of a temple was in front of the west cave. It is the mania for making the temple cover too large a space, and the desire to show that all its parts were exactly balanced on either side, and that this triangular shaped sanctuary culminated in a round temple, this it is that has caused so much trouble with the topography of the city. The temple, as it really is, was larger perhaps than any other in Latium, and certainly as imposing.

Delbrueck did not see that there was a real communication between the caves along the so-called cryptoporticus. There is a window-like hole, now walled up, in the east cave at the top, and it opened out upon the second story of the cryptoporticus, as Marucchi saw.[110] So there was an unseen means of getting from one cave to the other. This probably proves that suppliants at one shrine went to the other and were there convinced of the power of the goddess by seeing the same priest or something which they themselves had offered at the first shrine. It certainly proves that both caves were connected with the rites having to do with the proper obtaining of lots from Fortuna, and that this communication between the caves was unknown to any but the temple servants.

There are some other inscriptions not noticed by Delbrueck which mention the ædes,[111] and bear on the question in hand. One inscription found in the Via delle Monache[112] shows that in connection with the sedes Fortunæ were a manceps and three cellarii. This is an inscription of the last of the second or the first of the third century A.D.,[113] when both lower and upper temples were in very great favor. It shows further that only the lower temple is meant, for the number is too small to be applicable to the great upper temple, and it also shows that ædes, means the temple building itself and not the whole precinct. There is also an inscription, now in the floor of the cathedral, that mentions ædes. Its provenience is noteworthy.[114] There were other buildings, however, belonging to the precinct of the lower temple, as is shown by the remains today.[115] That there was more than one sacred building is also shown by inscriptions which mention ædes sacræ,[116] though these may refer of course to the upper temple as well.

There are yet two inscriptions of importance, one of which mentions a porticus, the other an ædes et porticus.[117] The second of these inscriptions belongs to a time not much later than the founding of the colony. It tells that certain work was done by decree of the decuriones, and it can hardly refer to the ancient lower temple, but must mean either the upper one, or still another out on the new forum, for there is where the stone is reported to have been found. The first inscription records a work of some consequence done by a woman in remembrance of her husband.[118] There are no remains to show that the forum below the town had any temple of such consequence, so it seems best to refer both these inscriptions to the upper temple, which, as we know, was rich in marble.[119]

Now after having brought together all the usages of the word ædes in its application to the temple of Præneste, it seems that Delbrueck has very small foundation for his argument which assumes as settled the exact meaning and location of the ædes Fortunæ.

From the temple itself we turn now to a brief discussion of a space on the tufa wall which helps to face the cave on the west. This is a smoothed surface which shows a narrow cornice ledge above it, and a narrow base below. In it are a number of irregularly driven holes. Delbrueck calls it a votive niche,[120] and says that the "viele regellos verstreute Nagelloecher" are due to nails upon which votive offerings were suspended.

This seems quite impossible. The holes are much too irregular to have served such a purpose. The holes show positively that they were made by nails which held up a slab of some kind, perhaps of marble, on which were displayed the replies from the goddess[121] which were too long to be given by means of the lettered blocks (sortes). Most likely, however, it was a marble slab or bronze tablet which contained the lex templi, and was something like the tabula Veliterna.[122]

On the floor of the two caves were two very beautiful mosaics, one of which is now in the Barberini palace, the other, which is in a sadly mutilated condition, still on the floor of the west cave. The date of these mosaics has been a much discussed question. Marucchi puts it at the end of the second century A.D., while Delbrueck makes it the early part of the first century B.C., and thinks the mosaics were the gift of Sulla. Delbrueck does not make his point at all, and Marucchi is carried too far by a desire to establish a connection at Præneste between Fortuna and Isis.[123] Not to go into a discussion of the date of the Greek lettering which gives the names of the animals portrayed in the finer mosaic, nor the subject of the mosaic itself,[124] the inscription given above[118] should help to settle the date of the mosaic. Under Claudius, between the years 51 and 54 A.D., a portico was decorated with marble and a coating of marble facing. That this was a very splendid ornamentation is shown by the fact that it is mentioned so particularly in the inscription. And if in 54 A.D. marble and marble facing were things so worthy of note, then certainly one hundred and thirty years earlier there was no marble mosaic floor in Præneste like the one under discussion, which is considered the finest large piece of Roman mosaic in existence. And it was fifty years later than the date Delbrueck wishes to assign to this mosaic, before marble began to be used in any great profusion in Rome, and at this time Præneste was not in advance of Rome. The mosaic, therefore, undoubtedly dates from about the time of Hadrian, and was probably a gift to the city when he built himself a villa below the town.[125]

Finally, a word with regard to the ærarium. This is under the temple of Fortuna, but is not built with any regard to the facade of the temple above. The inscription on the back wall of the chamber is earlier than the time of Sulla,[126] and the position of this little vault[127] shows that it was a treasury connected with the basilica, indeed its close proximity about makes it part of that building and proves that it was the storehouse for public funds and records. It occupied a very prominent place, for it was at the upper end of the old forum, directly in front of the Sacra Via that came up past the basilica from the Porta Triumphalis. The conclusion of the whole matter is that the earliest city forum grew up on the terrace in front of the place where the mysterious lots had leaped out of the living rock. A basilica was built in a prominent place in the northwest corner of the forum. Later, another wonderful cave was discovered or made, and at such a distance from the first one that a temple in front of it would have a facing on the forum beyond the basilica, and this also gave a space of ground which was leveled off into a terrace above the basilica and the forum, and made into a sacred precinct. Because the basilica occupied the middle front of the temple property, the temple was made to face west along the terrace, toward the more ancient cave. The sacred precinct in front of the temple and between the caves was enclosed, and had no entrance except at the west end where the Sacra Via ended, which was in front of the west cave. Before the temple, facing the sacred inclosure was the pronaos mentioned in the inscription above,[128] and along each side of this inclosure ran a row of columns, and probably one also on the west side. Both caves and the temple were consecrated to the service of Fortuna Primigenia, the tutelary goddess of Præneste. Both caves and an earlier temple, which occupied part of the site of the present one, belong to the early life of Præneste.

Sulla built a huge temple on the second terrace higher than the old temple, but its fame and sanctity were never comparable to its beauty and its pretensions.[129]

THE EPIGRAPHICAL TOPOGRAPHY OF PRÆNESTE.

ÆDICULA, C.I.L., XIV, 2908.

From the provenience of the inscription this building, not necessarily a sacred one (Dessau), was one of the many structures on the site of the new Forum below the town.

PUBLICA ÆDIFICIA, C.I.L., XIV, 2919, 3032.

Barbarus Pompeianus about 227 A.D. restored a number of public buildings which had begun to fall to pieces. A mensor æd(ificiorum) (see Dict. under sarcio) is mentioned in C.I.L., XIV, 3032.

ÆDES ET PORTICUS, C.I.L., XIV, 2980.

See discussion of temple, page 42.

ÆDES, C.I.L., XIV, 2864, 2867, 3007.

See discussion of temple, page 42.

ÆDES SACRÆ, C.I.L., XIV, 2922, 4091, 9== Annali dell'Inst., 1855, p. 86.

See discussion of temple, page 42.

ÆRARIUM, C.I.L., XIV, 2975; Bull. dell'Inst., 1881, p. 207; Marucchi, Bull. dell'Inst., 1881, p. 252; Nibby, Analisi, II, p. 504; best and latest, Delbrueck, Hellenistische Bauten in Latium, I, p. 58.

The points worth noting are: that this ærarium is not built with reference to the temple above, and that it faces out on the public square. These points have been discussed more at length above, and will receive still more attention below under the caption "FORUM."

AMPHITHEATRUM, C.I.L., XIV, 3010, 3014; Juvenal, III, 173; Ovid, A.A., I, 103 ff.

The remains found out along the Valmontone road[130] coincide nearly enough with the provenience of the inscription to settle an amphitheatre here of late imperial date. The tradition of the death of the martyr S. Agapito in an amphitheatre, and the discovery of a Christian church on the Valmontone road, have helped to make pretty sure the identification of these ruins.[131]

We know also from an inscription that there was a gladiatorial school at Præneste.[132]

BALNEÆ, C.I.L., XIV, 3013, 3014 add.

The so-called nymphæum, the brick building below the Via degli Arconi, mentioned page 41, seems to have been a bath as well as a fountain, because of the architectural fragments found there[133] when it was turned into a mill by the Bonanni brothers. The reservoir mentioned above on page 41 must have belonged also to a bath, and so do the ruins which are out beyond the villa under which the modern cemetery now is. From their orientation they seem to belong to the villa. There were also baths on the hill toward Gallicano, as the ruins show.[134]

BYBLIOTHECÆ, C.I.L., XIV, 2916.

These seem to have been two small libraries of public and private law books.[135] They were in the Forum, as the provenience of the inscription shows.

CIRCUS, Cecconi, Storia di Palestrina, p. 75, n. 32.

Cecconi thought there was a circus at the bottom of the depression between Colle S. Martino and the hill of Præneste. The depression does have a suspiciously rounded appearance below the Franciscan grounds, but a careful examination made by me shows no trace of cutting in the rock to make a half circle for seats, no traces of any use of the slope for seats, and no ruins of any kind.

CULINA, C.I.L., XIV, 3002.

This was a building of some consequence. Two quæstors of the city bought a space of ground 148-1/2 by 16 feet along the wall, and superintended the building of a culina there. The ground was made public, and the whole transaction was done by decree of the senate, that is, it was done before the time of Sulla.

CURIA, C.I.L., XIV, 2924.

The fact that a statue was to be set up (ve)l ante curiam vel in porticibus for(i) would seem to imply that the curia was in the lower Forum. The inscription shows that these two places were undoubtedly the most desirable places that a statue could have. There is a possibility that the curia may be the basilica on the Corso terrace of the city. It has been shown that an open space existed in front of the basilica, and that in it there is at least one basis for a statue. Excavations[136] at the ruins which were once thought to be the curia of ancient Præneste showed instead of a hemicycle, a straight wall built on remains of a more ancient construction of rectangular blocks of tufa with three layers of pavement 4-1/2 feet below the level of the ground, under which was a tomb of brick construction, and lower still a wall of opus quadratum of tufa, certainly none of the remains belonging to a curia.

PLATE IV. The Sacra Via, and its turn round the upper end of the Basilica

FORUM, C.I.L., XIV, 3015.

The most ancient forum of Præneste was inside the city walls. It was in this forum that the statue of M. Anicius, the famous prætor, was set up.[137] The writers hitherto, however, have been entirely mistaken, in my opinion, as to the extent of the ancient forum. For the old forum was not an open space which is now represented by the Piazza Savoia of the modern town, as is generally accepted, but the ancient forum of Præneste was that piazza and the piazza Garibaldi and the space between them, now built over with houses, all combined. At the present time one goes down some steps in front of the cathedral, which was the basilica, to the Piazza Garibaldi, and it has been supposed that this open space belonged to a terrace below the Corso. But there was no lower terrace there. The upper part of the forum simply has been more deeply buried in debris than the lower part.

One needs only to see the new excavations at the upper end of the Piazza Savoia to realize that the present ground level of the piazza is nearly nine feet higher than the pavement of the old forum. The accompanying illustration (plate IV) shows the pavement, which is limestone, not lava, that comes up the slope along the east side of the basilica,[138] and turns round it to the west. A cippus stands at the corner to do the double duty of defining the limits of the basilica, and to keep the wheels of wagons from running up on the steps. It can be seen clearly that the lowest step is one stone short of the cippus, that the next step is on a level with the pavement at the cippus, and the next step level again with the pavement four feet beyond it. The same grade would give us about twelve or fifteen steps at the south end of the basilica, and if continued to the Piazza Garibaldi, would put us below the present level of that piazza. From this piazza on down through the garden of the Petrini family to the point where the existence of a Porta Triumphalis has been proved, the grade would not be even as steep as it was in the forum itself. Further, to show that the lower piazza is even yet accessible from the upper, despite its nine feet more of fill, if one goes to the east end of the Piazza Savoia he finds there instead of steps, as before the basilica, a street which leads down to the level of the Piazza Garibaldi, and although it begins at the present level of the upper piazza, it is not even now too steep for wagons. Again, one must remember that the opus quadratum wall which extends along the south side of the Corso does not go past the basilica, and also that there is a basis for a statue of some kind in front of the basilica on the level of the Piazza Garibaldi.

It is a question whether the ancient forum was entirely paved. The paving can be seen along the basilica, and it has been seen back of it,[139] but this pavement belongs to another hitherto unknown part of Præneste topography, namely, a SACRA VIA. An inscription to an aurufex de sacra via[140] makes certain that there was a road in Præneste to which this name was given. The inscription was found in the courtyard of the Seminary, which was the precinct of the temple of Fortuna. From the fact that this pavement is laid with blocks such as are always used in roads, from the cippus at the corner of the basilica to keep off wagon wheels, from the fact that this piece of pavement is in direct line from the central gate of the town, and last from the inscription and its provenience, I conclude that we have in this pavement a road leading directly from the Porta Triumphalis through the forum, alongside the basilica, then turning back of it and continuing round to the delubra and precinct of the temple of Fortuna Primigenia, and that this road is the SACRA VIA of Præneste.[141]

At the upper end of the forum under the south façade of the temple, an excavation was made in April 1907,[142] which is of great interest and importance in connection with the forum. In Plate V we see that there are three steps of tufa,[143] and observe that the space in front of them is not paved; also that the ascent to the right, which is the only way out of the forum at this corner, is too steep to have been ever more than for ascent on foot. But it is up this steep and narrow way[144] that every one had to go to reach the terrace above the temple, unless he went across to the west side of the city.

The steps just mentioned are not the beginning of an ascent to the temple, for there were but three, and besides there was no entrance to the temple on the south.[145] Nor was the earlier temple much lower than the later one, for in either case the foundation was the rock surface of the terrace and has not changed much. Although these steps are of an older construction than the steps of the basilica, yet they were not covered up in late imperial times as is shown by the brick construction in the plate. One is tempted to believe that there was a Doric portico below the engaged Corinthian columns of the south façade of the temple.[146] But all the pieces of Doric columns found belong to the portico of the basilica. Otherwise one might try to set up further argument for a portico, and even claim that here was the place that the statue was set up, ante curiam vel in por ticibus fori.[147] Again, these steps run far past the temple to the east, otherwise we might conclude that they were to mark the extent of temple property. The fact, however, that a road, the Sacra Via, goes round back of the basilica only to the left, forces us to conclude that these steps belong to the city, not to the temple in any way, and that they mark the north side of the ancient forum.

The new forum below the city is well enough attested by inscriptions found there mentioning statues and buildings in the forum. The tradition has continued that here on the level space below the town was the great forum. Inscriptions which have been found in different places on this tract of ground mention five buildings,[148] ten statues of public men,[149] the statue set up to the emperor Trajan on his birthday, September 18, 101 A.D.,[150] and one to the emperor Julian.[151] The discovery of two pieces of the Prænestine fasti in 1897 and 1903[152] also helps to locate the lower forum.[153]

PLATE V. The tufa steps at the upper end of the ancient Forum of Praeneste.

The forum inside the city walls was the forum of Præneste, the ally of Rome, the more pretentious one below the city was the forum of Præneste, the Roman colony of Sulla.

IUNONARIUM, C.I.L., XIV, 2867.

Delbrueck follows Preller[154] in making the Iunonarium a part of the temple of Fortuna. It seems strange to have a statue of Trivia dedicated in a Iunonarium, but it is stranger that there are no inscriptions among those from Præneste which mention Juno, except that the name alone appears on a bronze mirror and two bronze dishes,[155] and as the provenience of bronze is never certain, such inscriptions mean nothing. It seems that the Iunonarium must have been somewhere in the west end of the temple precinct of Fortuna.

KASA CUI VOCABULUM EST FULGERITA, C.I.L., XIV, 2934.

This is an inscription which mentions a property inside the domain of Præneste in a region, which in 385 A.D., was called regio Campania,[156] but it can not be located.

LACUS, C.I.L., XIV, 2998; Not. d. Scavi, 1902, p. 12. LAVATIO, C.I.L., XIV, 2978, 2979, 3015.

These three inscriptions were found in places so far from one another that they may well refer to three lavationes.

LUDUS, C.I.L., XIV, 3014.

See amphitheatrum.

MACELLUM, C.I.L., XIV, 2937, 2946.

These inscriptions were found along the Via degli Arconi, and from the fact that in 243 A.D. (C.I.L. XIV, 2972) there was a region (regio) by that name, I should conclude that the lower part of the town below the wall was called regio macelli. In Cecconi's time the city was divided into four quarters,[157] which may well represent ancient tradition.

MACERIA, C.I.L., XIV, 3314, 3340.

Cecconi, Storia di Palestrina, p. 87.

MASSA PRÆ(NESTINA), C.I.L., XIV, 2934.

MURUS, C.I.L., XIV, 3002.

See above, pages 22 ff.

PORTA TRIUMPHALIS, C.I.L., XIV, 2850.

See above, page 32.

PORTICUS, C.I.L., XIV, 2995.

See discussion of temple, page 42.

QUADRIGA, C.I.L., XIV, 2986.

SACRARIUM, C.I.L., XIV, 2900.

SCHOLA FAUSTINIANA, C.I.L., XIV, 2901; C.I.G., 5998.

Fernique (Étude sur Préneste, p. 119) thinks this the building the ruins of which are of brick and called a temple, near the Ponte dell' Ospedalato, but this is impossible. The date of the brick work is all much later than the date assigned to it by him, and much later than the name itself implies.

SEMINARIA A PORTA TRIUMPHALE, C.I.L., XIV, 2850.

This building was just inside the gate which was in the center of the south wall of Præneste, directly below the ancient forum and basilica.

SOLARIUM, C.I.L., XIV, 3323.

SPOLIARIUM, C.I.L., XIV, 3014.

See Amphitheatrum.

TEMPLUM SARAPIS, C.I.L., XIV, 2901.

TEMPLUM HERCULIS, C.I.L., XIV, 2891, 2892; Not. d. Scavi, 11 (1882-1883), p. 48.

This temple was a mile or more distant from the city, in the territory now known as Bocce di Rodi, and was situated on the little road which made a short cut between the two great roads, the Prænestina and the Labicana.

SACRA VIA, Not. d. Scavi, Ser. 5, 4 (1896), p. 49.

In the discussions on the temple and the forum, pages 42 and 54, I think it is proved that the Sacra Via of Præneste was the ancient road which extended from the Porta Triumphalis up through the Forum, past the Basilica and round behind it, to the entrance into the precinct and temple of Fortuna Primigenia.

VIA, C.I.L., XIV, 3001, 3343. Viam sternenda(m).

In inscription No. 3343 we have supra viam parte dex(tra), and from the provenience of the stone we get a proof that the old road which led out through the Porta S. Francesco was so well known that it was called simply "via."

CHAPTER II.
THE MUNICIPAL GOVERNMENT OF PRÆNESTE.

Præneste was already a rich and prosperous community, when Rome was still fighting for a precarious existence. The rapid development, however, of the Latin towns, and the necessity of mutual protection and advancement soon brought Rome and Præneste into a league with the other towns of Latium. Præneste because of her position and wealth was the haughtiest member of the newly made confederation, and with the more rapid growth of Rome became her most hated rival. Later, when Rome passed from a position of first among equals to that of mistress of her former allies, Præneste was her proudest and most turbulent subject.

From the earliest times, when the overland trade between Upper Etruria, Magna Græcia, and Lower Etruria came up the Liris valley, and touching Præneste and Tibur crossed the river Tiber miles above Rome, that energetic little settlement looked with longing on the city that commanded the splendid valley between the Sabine and Volscian mountains. Rome turned her conquests in the direction of her longings, but could get no further than Gabii. Præneste and Tibur were too strongly situated, and too closely connected with the fierce mountaineers of the interior,[158] and Rome was glad to make treaties with them on equal terms.

Rome, however, made the most of her opportunities. Her trade up and down the river increased, and at the same time brought her in touch with other nations more and more. Her political importance grew rapidly, and it was not long before she began to assume the primacy among the towns of the Latin league. This assumption of a leadership practically hers already was disputed by only one city. This was Præneste, and there can be no doubt but that if Præneste had possessed anything approaching the same commercial facilities in way of communication by water she would have been Rome's greatest rival. As late as 374 B.C. Præneste was alone an opponent worthy of Rome.[159]

As head of a league of nine cities,[160] and allied with Tibur, which also headed a small confederacy,[161] Præneste felt herself strong enough to defy the other cities of the league,[162] and in fact even to play fast and loose with Rome, as Rome kept or transgressed the stipulations of their agreements. Rome, however, took advantage of Præneste at every opportunity. She assumed control of some of her land in 338 B.C., on the ground that Præneste helped the Gauls in 390;[163] she showed her jealousy of Præneste by refusing to allow Quintus Lutatius Cerco to consult the lots there during the first Punic war.[164] This jealousy manifested itself again in the way the leader of a contingent from Præneste was treated by a Roman dictator[165] in 319 B.C. But while these isolated outbursts of jealousy showed the ill feeling of Rome toward Præneste, there is yet a stronger evidence of the fact that Præneste had been in early times more than Rome's equal, for through the entire subsequent history of the aggrandizement of Rome at the expense of every other town in the Latin League, there runs a bitterness which finds expression in the slurs cast upon Præneste, an ever-recurring reminder of the centuries of ancient grudge. Often in Roman literature Præneste is mentioned as the typical country town. Her inhabitants are laughed at because of their bad pronunciation, despised and pitied because of their characteristic combination of pride and rusticity. Yet despite the dwindling fortunes of the town she was able to keep a treaty with Rome on nearly equal terms until 90 B.C., the year in which the Julian law was passed.[166] Præneste scornfully refused Roman citizenship in 216 B.C., when it was offered.[167] This refusal Rome never forgot nor forgave. No Prænestine families seem to have been taken into the Roman patriciate, as were some from Alba Longa,[168] nor did Præneste ever send any citizens of note to Rome, who were honored as was Cato from Tusculum,[169] although one branch of the gens Anicia[170] did gain some reputation in imperial times. Rome and Præneste seemed destined to be ever at cross purposes, and their ancient rivalry grew to be a traditional dislike which remained mutual and lasting.

The continuance of the commercial and military rivalry because of Præneste's strategic position as key of Rome, and the religious rivalry due to the great fame of Fortuna Primigenia at Præneste, are continuous and striking historical facts even down into the middle ages. Once in 1297 and again in 1437 the forces of the Pope destroyed the town to crush the great Colonna family which had made Præneste a stronghold against the power of Rome.

There are a great many reasons why Præneste offers the best opportunity for a study of the municipal officers of a town of the Latin league. She kept a practical autonomy longer than any other of the league towns with the exception of Tibur, but she has a much more varied history than Tibur. The inscriptions of Præneste offer especial advantages, because they are numerous and cover a wide range. The great number of the old pigne inscriptions gives a better list of names of the citizens of the second century B.C. and earlier than can be found in any other Latin town.[171] Præneste also has more municipal fasti preserved than any other city, and this fact alone is sufficient reason for a study of municipal officers. In fact, the position which Præneste held during the rise and fall of the Latin League has distinct differences from that of any other town in the confederation, and these differences are to be seen in every stage of her history, whether as an ally, a municipium, or a colonia.

As an ally of Rome, Præneste did not have a curtailed treaty as did Alba Longa,[172] but one on equal terms (foedus æquum), such as was accorded to a sovereign state. This is proved by the right of exile which both Præneste and Tibur still retained until as late as 90 B.C.[173]

As a municipium, the rights of Præneste were shared by only one other city in the league. She was not a municipium which, like Lanuvium and Tusculum,[174] kept a separate state, but whose citizens, although called Roman citizens, were without right to vote, nor, on the other hand, was she in the class of municipia of which Aricia is a type, towns which had no vote in Rome, but were governed from there like a city ward.[175] Præneste, on the contrary, belonged to yet a third class. This was the most favored class of all; in fact, equality was implicit in the agreement with Rome, which was to the effect that when these cities joined the Roman state, the inhabitants were to be, first of all, citizens of their own states.[176] Præneste shared this extraordinary agreement with Rome with but one other Latin city, Tibur. The question whether or not Præneste was ever a municipium in the technical and constitutional sense of the word is apart from the present discussion, and will be taken up later.[177]

As a colony, Præneste has a different history from that of any other of the colonies founded by Sulla. Because of her stubborn defence, and her partisanship for Marius, her walls were razed and her citizens murdered in numbers almost beyond belief. Yet at a later time, Sulla with a revulsion of kindness quite characteristic of him, rebuilt the town, enlarged it, and was most generous in every way. The sentiment which attached to the famous antiquity and renown of Præneste was too strong to allow it to lie in ruins. Further, in colonies the most characteristic officers were the quattuorviri. Præneste, again different, shows no trace of such officers.

Indeed, at all times during the history of Latium, Præneste clearly had a city government different from that of any other in the old Latin League. For example, before the Social War[178] both Præneste and Tibur had ædiles and quæstors, but Tibur also had censors,[179] Præneste did not. Lavinium[180] and Præneste were alike in that they both had prætors. There were dictators in Aricia,[181] Lanuvium,[182] Nomentum,[183] and Tusculum,[184] but no trace of a dictator in Præneste.

The first mention of a magistrate from Præneste, a prætor, in 319 B.C, is due to a joke of the Roman dictator Papirius Cursor.[185] The prætor was in camp as leader of the contingent of allies from Præneste,[186] and the fact that a prætor was in command of the troops sent from allied towns[187] implies that another prætor was at the head of affairs at home. Another and stronger proof of the government by two prætors is afforded by the later duoviral magistracy, and the lack of friction under such an arrangement.

There is no reason to believe that the Latin towns took as models for their early municipal officers, the consuls at Rome, rather than to believe that the reverse was the case. In fact, the change in Rome to the name consuls from prætors,[188] with the continuance of the name prætor in the towns of the Latin League, would rather go to prove that the Romans had given their two chief magistrates a distinctive name different from that in use in the neighboring towns, because the more rapid growth in Rome of magisterial functions demanded official terminology, as the Romans began their "Progressive Subdivision of the Magistracy."[189] Livy says that in 341 B.C. Latium had two prætors,[190] and this shows two things: first, that two prætors were better adapted to circumstances than one dictator; second, that the majority of the towns had prætors, and had had them, as chief magistrates, and not dictators,[191] and that such an arrangement was more satisfactory. The Latin League had had a dictator[192] at its head at some time,[193] and the fact that these two prætors are found at the head of the league in 341 B.C. shows the deference to the more progressive and influential cities of the league, where prætors were the regular and well known municipal chief magistrates. Before Præneste was made a colony by Sulla, the governing body was a senate,[194] and the municipal officers were prætors,[195] ædiles,[196] and quæstors,[197] as we know certainly from inscriptions. In the literature, a prætor is mentioned in 319 B.C.,[198] in 216 B.C.,[199] and again in 173 B.C. implicitly, in a statement concerning the magistrates of an allied city.[200] In fact nothing in the inscriptions or in the literature gives a hint at any change in the political relations between Præneste and Rome down to 90 B.C., the year in which the lex Iulia was passed. If a dictator was ever at the head of the city government in Præneste, there are none of the proofs remaining, such as are found in the towns of the Alban Hills, in Etruria, and in the medix tuticus of the Sabellians. The fact that no trace of the dictator remains either in Tibur or Præneste seems to imply that these two towns had better opportunities for a more rapid development, and that both had prætors at a very early period.[201]

However strongly the weight of probabilities make for proof in the endeavor to find out what the municipal government of Præneste was, there are a certain number of facts that can now be stated positively. Before 90 B.C. the administrative officers of Præneste were two prætors,[202] who had the regular ædiles and quæstors as assistants. These officers were elected by the citizens of the place. There was also a senate, but the qualifications and duties of its members are uncertain. Some information, however, is to be derived from the fact that both city officers and senate were composed in the main of the local nobility.[203]

An important epoch in the history of Præneste begins with the year 91 B.C. In this year the dispute over the extension of the franchise to Italy began again, and the failure of the measure proposed by the tribune M. Livius Drusus led to an Italian revolt, which soon assumed a serious aspect. To mitigate or to cripple this revolt (the so-called Social or Marsic war), a bill was offered and passed in 90 B.C. This was the famous law (lex Iulia) which applied to all Italian states that had not revolted, or had stopped their revolt, and it offered Roman citizenship (civitas) to all such states, with, however, the remarkable provision, IF THEY DESIRED IT.[204] At all events, this law either did not meet the needs of the occasion, or some of the allied states showed no eagerness to accept Rome's offer. Within a few months after the lex Iulia had gone into effect, which was late in the year 90, the lex Plautia Papiria was passed, which offered Roman citizenship to the citizens (cives et incolæ) of the federated cities, provided they handed in their names within sixty days to the city prætor in Rome.[205]

There is no unanimity of opinion as to the status of Præneste in 90 B.C. The reason is twofold. It has never been shown whether Præneste at this time belonged technically to the Latins (Latini) or to the allies (foederati), and it is not known under which of the two laws just mentioned she took Roman citizenship. In 338 B.C., after the close of the Latin war, Præneste and Tibur made either a special treaty[206] with Rome, as seems most likely, or one in which the old status quo was reaffirmed. In 268 B.C. Præneste lost one right of federated cities, that of coinage,[207] but continued to hold the right of a sovereign city, that of exile (ius exilii) in 171 B.C.,[208] in common with Tibur and Naples,[209] and on down to the year 90 at any rate (see note 9). It is to be remembered too that in the year 216 B.C., after the heroic deeds of the Prænestine cohort at Casilinum, the inhabitants of Præneste were offered Roman citizenship, and that they refused it.[210] Now if the citizens of Præneste accepted Roman citizenship in 90 B.C., under the conditions of the Julian law (lex Iulia de civitate sociis danda), then they were still called allies (socii) at that time.[211] But that the provision in the law, namely, citizenship, if the allies desired it, did not accomplish its purpose, is clear from the immediate passage in 89 of the lex Plautia-Papiria.[212] Probably there was some change of phraseology which was obnoxious in the Iulia. The traditional touchiness and pride of the Prænestines makes it sure that they resisted Roman citizenship as long as they could, and it seems more likely that it was under the provision of the Plautia-Papiria than under those of the Iulia that separate citizenship in Præneste became a thing of the past. Two years later, in 87 B.C., when, because of the troubles between the two consuls Cinna and Octavius,

Cinna had been driven from Rome, he went out directly to Præneste and Tibur, which had lately been received into citizenship,[213] tried to get them to revolt again from Rome, and collected money for the prosecution of the war. This not only shows that Præneste had lately received Roman citizenship, but implies also that Rome thus far had not dared to assume any control of the city, or the consul would not have felt so sure of his reception.

WAS PRÆNESTE A MUNICIPIUM?

Just what relation Præneste bore to Rome between 90 or 89 B.C., when she accepted Roman citizenship, and 82 B.C. when Sulla made her a colony, is still an unsettled question. Was Præneste made a municipium by Rome, did Præneste call herself a municipium, or, because the rights which she enjoyed and guarded as an ally (civitas foederata) had been so restricted and curtailed, was she called and considered a municipium by Rome, but allowed to keep the empty substance of the name of an allied state?

During the development which followed the gradual extension of Roman citizenship to the inhabitants of Italy, because of the increase of the rights of autonomy in the colonies, and the limitation of the rights formerly enjoyed by the cities which had belonged to the old confederation or league (foederati), there came to be small difference between a colonia and a municipium. While the nominal difference seems to have still held in legal parlance, in the literature the two names are often interchanged.[214] Mommsen-Marquardt say[215] that in 90 B.C. under the conditions of the lex Iulia Præneste became a municipium of the type which kept its own citizenship (ut municipes essent suæ cuiusque civitatis).[216] But if this were true, then Præneste would have come under the jurisdiction of the city prætor (prætor urbanus) in Rome, and there would be præfects to look after cases for him. Præneste has a very large body of inscriptions which extend from the earliest to the latest times, and which are wider in range than those of any other town in Latium outside Rome. But no inscription mentions a præfect and here under the circumstances the argumentum ex silentio is of real constructive value, and constitutes circumstantial evidence of great weight.[217] Præneste had lost her ancient rights one after the other, but it is sure that she clung the longest to the separate property right. Now the property in a municipium is not considered as Roman, a result of the old sovereign state idea, as given by the ius Quiritium and ius Gabinorum, although Mommsen says this had no real practical value.[218] So whether Præneste received Roman citizenship in 90 or in 89 B.C. the spirit of her past history makes it certain that she demanded a clause which gave specific rights to the old federated states, such as had always been in her treaty with Rome.[219] There seems to have been no such clause in the lex Iulia of 90 B.C., and this fact gives still another reason, in addition to the ones mentioned, to conclude that Præneste probably took citizenship in 89 under the lex Plautia-Papiria. The extreme cruelty which Sulla used toward Præneste,[220] and the great amount of its land[221] that he took for his soldiers when he colonized the place, show that Sulla not only punished the city because it had sided with Marius, but that the feeling of a Roman magistrate was uppermost, and that he was now avenging traditional grievances, as well as punishing recent obstreperousness.

There seems to be, however, very good reasons for saying that Præneste never became a municipium in the strict legal sense of the word. First, the particular officials who belong to a municipium, præfects and quattuorvirs, are not found at all;[222] second, the use of the word municipium in literature in connection with Præneste is general, and means simply "town";[223] third, the fact that Præneste, along with Tibur, had clung so jealously to the title of federated state (civitas foederata) from some uncertain date to the time of the Latin rebellion, and more proudly than ever from 338 to 90 B.C., makes it very unlikely that so great a downfall of a city's pride would be passed over in silence; fourth and last, the fact that the Prænestines asked the emperor Tiberius to give them the status of a municipium,[224] which he did,[225] but it seems (see note 60) with no change from the regular city officials of a colony,[226] shows clearly that the Prænestines simply took advantage of the fact that Tiberius had just recovered from a severe illness at Præneste[227] to ask him for what was merely an empty honor. It only salved the pride of the Prænestines, for it gave them a name which showed a former sovereign federated state, and not the name of a colony planted by the Romans.[228] The cogency of this fourth reason will bear elaboration. Præneste would never have asked for a return to the name municipium if it had not meant something. At the very best she could not have been a real municipium with Roman citizenship longer than seven years, 89 to 82 B.C., and that at a very unsettled time, nor would an enforced taking of the status of a municipium, not to mention the ridiculously short period which it would have lasted, have been anything to look back to with such pride that the inhabitants would ask the emperor Tiberius for it again. What they did ask for was the name municipium as they used and understood it, for it meant to them everything or anything but colonia.

Let us now sum up the municipal history of Præneste down to 82 B.C. when she was made a Roman colony by Sulla. Præneste, from the earliest times, like Rome, Tusculum, and Aricia, was one of the chief cities in the territory known as Ancient Latium. Like these other cities, Præneste made herself head of a small league,[229] but unlike the others, offers nothing but comparative probability that she was ever ruled by kings or dictators. So of prime importance not only in the study of the municipal officers of

Præneste, but also in the question of Præneste's relationship to Rome, is the fact that the evidence from first to last is for prætors as the chief executive officers of the Prænestine state (respublica), with their regular attendant officers, ædiles and quæstors; all of whom probably stood for office in the regular succession (cursus honorum). Above these officers was a senate, an administrative or advisory body. But although Præneste took Roman citizenship either in 90 or 89 B.C.,[213] it seems most likely that she was not legally termed a municipium, but that she came in under some special clause, or with some particular understanding, whereby she kept her autonomy, at least in name. Præneste certainly considered herself a federate city, on the old terms of equality with Rome, she demanded and partially retained control of her own land, and preserved her freedom from Rome in the matter of city elections and magistrates.

PRÆNESTE AS A COLONY.

From the time of Sulla to the establishment of the monarchy, the expropriation of territory for discharged soldiers found its expression in great part in the change from Italian cities to colonies,[230] and of the colonies newly made by Sulla, Præneste was one. The misfortunes that befell Præneste, because she seemed doomed to be on the losing side in quarrels, were never more disastrously exemplified than in the punishment inflicted upon her by Sulla, because she had taken the side of Marius. Thousands of her citizens were killed (see note 220), her fortifications were thrown down, a great part of her territory was taken and given to Sulla's soldiers, who were the settlers of his new-made colony. At once the city government of Præneste changed. Instead of a senate, there was now a decuria (decuriones, ordo); instead of prætors, duovirs with judicial powers (iure dicundo), in short, the regular governmental officialdom for a Roman colony. The city offices were filled partly by the new colonists, and the new government which was forced upon her was so thoroughly established, that Præneste remained a colony as long as her history can be traced in the inscriptions. As has been said, in the time of Tiberius she got back an empty title, that of municipium, but it had been nearly forgotten again by Hadrian's time.

There are several unanswered questions which arise at this point. What was the distribution of offices in the colony after its foundation; what regulation, if any, was there as to the proportion of officials to the new make up of the population; and what and who were the quinquennial duovirs? From the proportionately large fragments of municipal fasti left from Præneste it will be possible to reach some conclusions that may be of future value.

THE DISTRIBUTION OF OFFICES.

The beginning of this question comes from a passage in Cicero,[231] which says that the Sullan colonists in Pompeii were preferred in the offices, and had a status of citizenship better than that of the old inhabitants of the city. Such a state of affairs might also seem natural in a colony which had just been deprived of one third of its land, and had had forced upon it as citizens a troop of soldiers who naturally would desire to keep the city offices as far as possible in their own control.[232] Dessau thinks that because this unequal state of citizenship was found in Pompeii, which was a colony of Sulla's, it must have been found also in Præneste, another of his colonies.[233] Before entering into the question of whether or not this can be proved, it will be well to mention three probable reasons why Dessau is wrong in his contention. The first, an argumentum ex silentio, is that if there was trouble in Pompeii between the old inhabitants and the new colonists then the same would have been true in Præneste! As it was so close to Rome, however, the trouble would have been much better known, and certainly Cicero would not have lost a chance to bring the state of affairs at Præneste also into a comparison. Second, the great pains Sulla took to rebuild the walls of Præneste, to lay out a new forum, and especially to make such an extensive enlargement and so many repairs of the temple of Fortuna Primigenia, show that his efforts were not entirely to please his new colonists, but just as much to try to defer to the wishes and civic pride of the old settlers. Third, the fact that a great many of the old inhabitants were left, despite the great slaughter at the capture of the city, is shown by the frequent recurrence in later inscriptions of the ancient names of the city, and by the fact that within twenty years the property of the soldier colonists had been bought up,[234] and the soldiers had died, or had moved to town, or reenlisted for foreign service. Had there been much trouble between the colonists and the old inhabitants, or had the colonists taken all the offices, in either case they would not have been so ready to part with their land, which was a sort of patent to citizenship.

It is possible now to push the inquiry a point further. Dessau has already seen[235] that in the time of Augustus members of the old families were again in possession of many municipal offices, but he thinks the Prænestines did not have as good municipal rights as the colonists in the years following the establishment of the colony. There are six inscriptions[236] which contain lists more or less fragmentary of the magistrates of Præneste, the duovirs, the ædiles, and the quæstors. Two of these inscriptions can be dated within a few years, for they show the election of Germanicus and Drusus Cæsar, and of Nero and Drusus, the sons of Germanicus, to the quinquennial duovirate.[237] Two others[238] are certainly pieces of the same fasti because of several peculiarities,[239] and one other, a fragment, belongs to still another calendar.[240] It will first be necessary to show that these last-mentioned inscriptions can be referred to some time not much later than the founding of the colony at Præneste by Sulla, before any use can be made of the names in the list to prove anything about the early distribution of officers in the colony. Two of these inscriptions[238] should be placed, I think, very early in the annals of the colony. They show a list of municipal officers whose names, with a single exception, which will be accounted for later, have only prænomen and nomen, a way of writing names which was common to the earlier inhabitants of Præneste, and which seems to have made itself felt here in the names of the colonists.[241] Again, from the fact that in the only place in the inscriptions where the quinquennialship is mentioned, it is the simple term, without the prefixed duoviri. In the later inscriptions from imperial times,[237] both forms are found, while in the year 31 A.D. in the municipal fasti of Nola[242] are found II vir(i) iter(um) q(uinquennales), and in 29 B.C. in the fasti from Venusia,[243] officials with the same title, duoviri quinquennales, which show that the officers of the year in which the census was taken were given both titles. Marquardt makes this a proof that the quinquennial title shows nothing more than a function of the regular duovir.[244] It is certain too that after the passage of the lex Iulia in 45 B.C., that the census was taken in the Italian towns at the same time as in Rome, and the reports sent to the censor in Rome.[245] This duty was performed by the duovirs with quinquennial power, also often called censorial power.[246] The inscriptions under consideration, then, would seem to date certainly before 49 B.C.

Another reason for placing these inscriptions in the very early days of the colony is derived from the use of names. In this list of officials[247] there is a duovir by the name of P. Cornelius, and another whose name is lost except for the cognomen, Dolabella, but he can be no other than a Cornelius, for this cognomen belongs to that family.[248] Early in the life of the colony, immediately after its settlement, during the repairs and rebuilding of the city's monuments,[249] while the soldiers from Sulla's army were the new citizens of the town, would be the time to look for men in the city offices whose election would have been due to Sulla, or would at least appear to have been a compliment to him. Sulla was one of the most famous of the family of the Cornelii, and men of the gens Cornelia might well have expected preferment during the early years of the colony. That such was the case is shown here by the recurrence of the name Cornelius in the list of municipal officers in two succeeding years. Now if the name "Cornelia" grew to be a name in great disfavor in Præneste, the reason would be plain enough. The destruction of the town, the loss of its ancient liberties, and the change in its government, are more than enough to assure hatred of the man who had been the cause of the disasters. And there is proof too that the Prænestines did keep a lasting dislike to the name "Cornelia." There are many inscriptions of Præneste which show the names (nomina) Ælia, Antonia, Aurelia, Claudia, Flavia, Iulia, Iunia, Marcia, Petronia, Valeria, among others, but besides the two Cornelii in this inscription under consideration, and one other[250] mentioned in the fragment above (see note 83), there are practically no people of that name found in Præneste,[251] and the name is frequent enough in other towns of the old Latin league. From these reasons, namely, the way in which only prænomina and nomina are used, the simple, earlier use of quinquennalis, and especially the appearance of the name Cornelius here, and never again until in the late empire, it follows that the names of the municipal officers of Præneste given in these inscriptions certainly date between 81 and 50 B.C.[252]

THE REGULATIONS ABOUT OFFICIALS.

The question now arises whether the new colonists had better rights legally than the old citizens, and whether they had the majority of votes and elected city officers from their own number. The inscriptions with which we have to deal are both fragments of lists of city officers, and in the longer of the two, one gives the officers for four years, the corresponding column for two years and part of a third. A Dolabella, who belongs to the gens Cornelia, as we have seen, heads the list as duovir. The ædile for the same year is a certain Rotanius.[253] This name is not found in the sepulchral inscriptions of the city of Rome, nor in the inscriptions of Præneste except in this one instance. This man is certainly one of the new colonists, and probably a soldier from North Italy.[254] Both the quæstors of the same year are given. They are M. Samiarius and Q. Flavius. Samiarius is one of the famous old names of Præneste.[255] In the same way, the duovirs of the next year, C. Messienus and P. Cornelius, belong, the one to Præneste, the other to the colonists,[256] and just such an arrangement is also found in the ædiles, Sex. Cæsius being a Prænestine[257], L. Nassius a colonist. Q. Caleius and C. Sertorius, the quæstors of the same year, do not appear in the inscriptions of Præneste except here, and it is impossible to say more than that Sertorius is a good Roman name, and Caleius a good north Italian one.[258] C. Salvius and T. Lucretius, duovirs for the next year, the recurrence of Salvius in another inscription,[259] L. Curtius and C. Vibius, the ædiles,—Statiolenus and C. Cassius, the quæstors, show the same phenomenon, for it seems quite possible from other inscriptional evidence to claim Salvius, Vibius,[260] and Statiolenus[261] as men from the old families of Præneste. The quinquennalis for the next year, M. Petronius, has a name too widely prevalent to allow any certainty as to his native place, but the nomen Petronia and Ptronia is an old name in Præneste.[262] In the second column of the inscription, although the majority of the names there seem to belong to the new colonists, as those in the first column do to the old settlers, there are two names, Q. Arrasidius and T. Apponius, which do not make for the argument either way.[263] In the smaller fragment there are but six names: M. Decumius and L. Ferlidius, C. Paccius and C. Ninn(ius), C. Albinius and Sex. Capivas, but from these one gets only good probabilities. The nomen Decumia is well attested in Præneste before the time of Sulla.[264] In fact the same name, M. Decumius, is among the old pigne inscriptions.[265] Paccia has been found this past year in Prænestine territory, and may well be an old Prænestine name, for the inscriptions of a family of the name Paccia have come to light at Gallicano.[266] Capivas is at least not a Roman name,[267] but from its scarcity in other places can as well be one of the names that are so frequent in Præneste, which show Etruscan or Sabine formation, and which prove that before Sulla's time the city had a great many inhabitants who had come from Etruria and from back in the Sabine mountains. Ninnius[268] is a name not found elsewhere in the Latian towns, but the name belonged to the nobility near Capua,[269] and is found also in Pompeii[270] and Puteoli.[271] It seems a fair supposition to make at the outset, as we have seen that various writers on Præneste have done, that the new colonists would try to keep the highest office to themselves, at any rate, particularly the duovirate. But a study of the names, as has been the case with the less important officers, fails even to bear this out.[272] These lists of municipal officers show a number of names that belong with certainty to the older families of Præneste, and thus warrant the statement that the colonists did not have better rights than the old settlers, and that not even in the duovirate, which held an effective check (maior potestas)[273] on the ædiles and quæstors, can the names of the new colonists be shown to outnumber or take the place of the old settlers.

THE QUINQUENNALES.

There remains yet the question in regard to the men who filled the quinquennial office. We know that whether the officials of the municipal governments were prætors, ædiles, duovirs, or quattuorvirs, at intervals of five years their titles either were quinquennales,[274] or had that added to them, and that this title implied censorial duties.[275] It has also been shown that after 46 B.C. the lex Iulia compelled the census in the various Roman towns to be taken by the proper officers in the same year that it was done in Rome. This implies that the taking of the census had been so well established a custom that it was a long time before Rome itself had cared to enact a law which changed the year of census taking in those towns which had not of their own volition made their census contemporaneous with that in Rome.

That the duration of the quinquennial office was one year is certain,[276] that it was eponymous is also sure,[277] but whether the officers who performed these duties every five years did so in addition to holding the highest office of the year, or in place of that honor, is a question not at all satisfactorily answered. That is, were the men who held the quinquennial office the men who would in all probability have stood for the duovirate in the regular succession of advance in the round of offices (cursus honorum), or did the government at Rome in some way, either directly or indirectly, name the men for the highest office in that particular year when the census was to be taken? That is, again, were quinquennales elected as the other city officials were, or were they appointed by Rome, or were they merely designated by Rome, and then elected in the proper and regular way by the citizens of the towns?

At first glance it seems most natural to suppose that Rome would want exact returns from the census, and might for that reason try to dictate the men who were to take it, for on the census had been based always the military taxes, contingents, etc.[278] The first necessary inquiry is whether the quinquennales were men who previously had held office as quæstors or ædiles, and the best place to begin such a search is in the municipal calendars (fasti magistratuum municipalium), which give the city officials with their rank.

There are fragments left of several municipal fasti; the one which gives the longest unbroken list is that from Venusia,[279] which gives the full list of the city officials of the years 34-29 B.C., and the ædiles of 35, and both the duovirs and prætors of the first half of 28 B.C. In 29 B.C., L. Oppius and L. Livius were duoviri quinquennales. These are both good old Roman names, and stand out the more in contrast with Narius, Mestrius, Plestinus, and Fadius, the ædiles and quæstors. Neither of these quinquennales had held any office in the five preceding years at all events. One of the two quæstors of the year 33 B.C. is a L. Cornelius. The next year a L. Cornelius, with the greatest probability the same man, is præfect, and again in the year 30 he is duovir. Also in the year 32 L. Scutarius is quæstor, and in the last half of 31 is duovir. C. Geminius Niger is ædile in 30, and duovir in 28. So what we learn is that a L. Cornelius held the quæstorship one year, was a præfect the next, and later a regularly elected duovir; that L. Scutarius went from quæstor one year to duovir the next, without an intervening office, and but a half year of intervening time; and that C. Geminius Niger was successively ædile and duovir with a break of one year between.

The fasti of Nola[280] give the duovirs and ædiles for four years, 29-32 A.D., but none of the ædiles mentioned rose to the duovirate within the years given. Nor do we get any help from the fasti of Interamna Lirenatis[281] or Ostia,[282] so the only other calendar we have to deal with is the one from Præneste, the fragments of which have been partially discussed above.

The text of that piece[283] which dates from the first years of Tiberius' reign is so uncertain that one gets little information from it. But certainly the M. Petronius Rufus who is præfect for Drusus Cæsar is the same as the Petronius Rufus who in another place is duovir. The name of C. Dindius appears twice also, once with the office of ædile, but two years later seemingly as ædile again, which must be a mistake. M. Cominius Bassus is made quinquennalis by order of the senate, and also made præfect for Germanicus and Drusus Cæsar in their quinquennial year. He is not found in any other inscription, and is otherwise unknown.[284] The only other men who attained the quinquennial rank in Præneste were M. Petronius,[285] and some man with the cognomen Minus,[286] neither of whom appears anywhere else. A man with the cognomen Sedatus is quæstor in one year, and without holding other office is made præfect to the sons of Germanicus, Nero and Drusus, who were nominated quinquennales two years later.[287] There is no positive proof in any of the fasti that any quinquennalis was elected from one of the lower magistrates. There is proof that duovirs were elected, who had been ædiles or quæstors. Also it has been shown that in two cases men who had been quæstors were made præfects, that is, appointees of people who had been nominated quinquennales as an honor, and who had at once appointed præfects to carry out their duties.

Another question of importance rises here. Who were the quinquennales? They were not always inhabitants of the city to the office of which they had been nominated, as has been shown in the cases of Drusus and Germanicus Cæsar, and Nero and Drusus the sons of Germanicus, nominated or elected quinquennales at Præneste, and represented in both cases by præfects appointed by them.[288]

From Ostia comes an inscription which was set up by the grain measurers' union to Q. Petronius Q.f. Melior, etc.,[289] prætor of a small town some ten miles from Ostia, and also quattuorvir quinquennalis of Fæsulæ, a town above Florence, which seems to show that he was sent to Fæsulæ as a quinquennalis, for the honor which he had held previously was that of prætor in Laurentum.

At Tibur, in Hadrian's time, a L. Minicius L.f. Gal. Natalis Quadromius Verus, who had held offices previously in Africa, in Moesia, and in Britain, was made quinquennalis maximi exempli. It seems certain that he was not a resident of Tibur, and since he was not appointed as præfect by Hadrian, it seems quite reasonable to think that either the emperor had a right to name a quinquennalis, or that he was asked to name one,[290] when one remembers the proximity of Hadrian's great villa, and the deference the people of Tibur showed the emperor. There is also in Tibur an inscription to a certain Q. Pompeius Senecio, etc.—(the man had no less than thirty-eight names), who was an officer in Asia in 169 A.D., a præfect of the Latin games (præfectus feriarum Latinarum), then later a quinquennalis of Tibur, after which he was made patron of the city (patronus municipii).[291] A Roman knight, C. Æmilius Antoninus, was first quinquennalis, then patronus municipii at Tibur.[292]

N. Cluvius M'. f.[293] was a quattuorvir at Caudium, a duovir at Nola, and a quattuorvir quinquennalis at Capua, which again shows that a quinquennalis need not have been an official previously in the town in which he held the quinquennial office.

C. Mænius C.f. Bassus[294] was ædile and quattuorvir at Herculaneum and then after holding the tribuneship of a legion is found next at Præneste as a quinquennalis.

M. Vettius M.f. Valens[295] is called in an inscription duovir quinquennalis of the emperor Trajan, which shows not an appointment from the emperor in his place, for that would have been as a præfect, but rather that the emperor had nominated him, as an imperial right. This man held a number of priestly offices, was patron of the colony of Ariminum, and is called optimus civis.

Another inscription shows plainly that a man who had been quinquennalis in his own home town was later made quinquennalis in a colony founded by Augustus, Hispellum.[296] This man, C. Alfius, was probably nominated quinquennalis by the emperor.

C. Pompilius Cerialis,[297] who seems to have held only one other office, that of præfect to Drusus Cæsar in an army legion, was duovir iure dicundo quinquennalis in Volaterræ.

M. Oppius Capito was not only quinquennalis twice at Auximum, patron of that and another colony, but he was patron of the municipium of Numana, and also quinquennalis.[298]

Q. Octavius L.f. Sagitta was twice quinquennalis at Superæquum, and held no other offices.[299]

Again, particularly worthy of notice is the fact that when L. Septimius L.f. Calvus, who had been ædile and quattuorvir at Teate Marrucinorum, was given the quinquennial rights, it was of such importance that it needed especial mention, and that such mention was made by a decree of the city senate,[300] shows clearly that such a method of getting a quinquennalis was out of the ordinary.

M. Nasellius Sabinus of Beneventum[301] has the title Augustalis duovir quinquennalis, and no other title but that of præfect of a cohort.

C. Egnatius Marus of Venusia was flamen of the emperor Tiberius, pontifex, and præfectus fabrum, and three times duovir quinquennalis, which seems to show a deference to a man who was the priest of the emperor, and seems to preclude an election by the citizens after a regular term of other offices.[302]

Q. Laronius was a quinquennalis at Vibo Valentia by order of the senate, which again shows the irregularity of the choice.[303]

M. Træsius Faustus was quinquennalis of Potentia, but died an inhabitant of Atinæ in Lucania.[304]

M. Alleius Luccius Libella, who was ædile and duovir in Pompeii,[305] was not elected quinquennalis, but made præfectus quinquennalis, which implies appointment.

M. Holconius Celer was a priest of Augustus, and with no previous city offices is mentioned as quinquennalis-elect, which can perhaps as well mean nominated by the emperor, as designated by the popular vote.[306]

P. Sextilius Rufus,[307] ædile twice in Nola, is quinquennalis in Pompeii. As he was chosen by the old inhabitants of Nola to their senate, this would show that he belonged probably to the new settlers in the colony introduced by Augustus, and for some reason was called over also to Pompeii to take the quinquennial office.

L. Aufellius Rufus at Cales was advanced from the position of primipilus of a legion to that of quinquennalis, without having held any other city offices, but he was flamen of the deified emperor (Divus Augustus), and patron of the city.[308]

M. Barronius Sura went directly to quinquennalis without being ædile or quæstor, in Aquinum.[309]

Q. Decius Saturninus was a quattuorvir at Verona, but a quinquennalis at Aquinum.[310]

The quinquennial year seems to have been the year in which matters of consequence were more likely to be done than at other times.

In 166 A.D. in Ostia a dedication was of importance enough to have the names of both the consuls of the year and the duoviri quinquennales at the head of the inscription.[311]

The year that C. Cuperius and C. Arrius were quinquennales with censorial power (II vir c.p.q.) in Ostia, there was a dedication of some importance in connection with a tree that had been struck by lightning.[312]

In Gabii a decree in honor of the house of Domitia Augusta was passed in the year when there were quinquennales.[313]

In addition to the fact that the emperors were sometimes chosen quinquennales, the consuls were too. M'. Acilius Glabrio, consul ordinarius of 152 A.D., was made patron of Tibur and quinquennalis designatus.[314]

On the other hand, against this array of facts, are others just as certain, if not so cogent or so numerous. From the inscriptions painted on the walls in Pompeii, we know that in the first century A.D. men were recommended as quinquennales to the voters. But although there seems to be a large list of such inscriptions, they narrow down a great deal, and in comparison with the number of duovirs, they are considerably under the proportion one would expect, for instead of being as 1 to 4, they are really only as 1 to 19.[315] What makes the candidacy for quinquennialship seem a new and unaccustomed thing is the fact that the appeals for votes which are painted here and there on the walls are almost all recommendations for just two men.[316]

There are quinquennales who were made patrons of the towns in which they held the office, but who held no other offices there (1); some who were both quæstors and ædiles or prætors (2); quinquennales of both classes again who were not made patrons (3, 4); præfects with quinquennial power (5); quinquennales who go in regular order through the quattuorviral offices (6); those who go direct to the quinquennial rank from the tribunate of the soldiers (7); and (8) a VERY FEW who have what seems to be the regular order of lower offices first, quæstor, ædile or prætor, duovir, and then quinquennalis.[317]

The sum of the facts collected is as follows: the quinquennales are proved to have been elective officers in Pompeii. The date, however, is the third quarter of the first century A.D., and the office may have been but recently thrown open to election, as has been shown. Quinquennales who have held other city offices are very, very few, and they appear in inscriptions of fairly late date.

On the other hand, many quinquennales are found who hold that office and no other in the city, men who certainly belong to other towns, many who from their nomination as patrons of the colony or municipium, are clearly seen to have held the quinquennial power also as an honor given to an outsider. In what municipal fasti we have, we find no quinquennalis whose name appears at all previously in the list of city officials.

The fact that the lex Iulia in 45 B.C. compelled the census to be taken everywhere else in the same year as in Rome shows at all events that the census had been taken in certain places at other times, whether with an implied supervision from Rome or not, and the later positive evidence that the emperors and members of the imperial family, and consuls, who were nominated quinquennales, always appointed præfects in their places, who with but an exception or two were not city officials previously, certainly tends to show that at some time the quinquennial office had been influenced in some way from Rome. The appointment of outside men as an honor would then be a survival of the custom of having outsiders for quinquennales, in many places doubtless a revival of a custom which had been in abeyance, to honor the imperial family.

In Præneste, as in other colonies, it seems reasonable that Rome would want to keep her hand on affairs to some extent. Rome imposed on the colonies their new kind of officials, and in the fixing of duties and rights, what is more likely than that Rome would reserve a voice in the choice of those officials who were to turn in the lists on which Rome had to depend for the census?

Rome always made different treaties and understandings with her allies; according to circumstances, she made different arrangements with different colonies; even Sulla's own colonies show a vast difference in the treatment accorded them, for the plan was to conciliate the old inhabitants if they were still numerous enough to make it worth while, and the gradual change is most clearly shown by its crystallization in the lex Iulia of 45 B.C.

The evidence seems to warrant the following conclusions in regard to the quinquennales: From the first they were the most important city officials; they were elected by the people from the first, but were men who had been recommended in some way, or had been indorsed beforehand by the central government in Rome; they were not necessarily men who had held office previously in the city to which they were elected quinquennales; with the spread of the feeling of real Roman citizenship the necessity for indorsement from Rome fell into abeyance; magistrates were elected who had every expectation of going through the series of municipal offices in the regular way to the quinquennialship; and the later election of emperors and others to the quinquennial office was a survival of the habitual realization that this most honorable of city offices had some connection with the central authority, whatever that happened to be, and was not an integral part of municipal self government.

Such are some of the questions which a study of the municipal officers of Præneste has raised. It would be both tedious and unnecessary to enumerate again the offices which were held in Præneste during her history, but an attempt to place such a list in a tabular way is made in the following pages.

ALPHABETICAL LIST OF THE MUNICIPAL OFFICERS OF PRÆNESTE.

NAME.	OFFICE.	C.I.L. (XIV.)
Drusus Cæsar Germanicus Cæsar	Quinq.	2964
Nero et Drusus Germanici filii	Quinq.	2965
Nero Cæsar, between 51-54 A.D.	IIvir Quinq.	2995
— Accius ... us	Q	2964
P. Acilius P.f. Paullus, 243 A.D.	Q. Æd. IIvir.	2972
L. Aiacius	Q	2964
C. Albinius	Æd (?)	2968
M. Albinius M.f.	Æd, IIvir, IIvir Quinq.	2974
M. Anicius (Livy VIII, 11, 4)	Pr.	
M. Anicius L.f. Baaso	Æd.	2975
P. Annius Septimus	IIvir.	4091, 1
(M). Antonius Subarus[318]	IIvir.	4091, 18
Aper, see Voesius.		
T. Aponius	Q	2966
P. Aquilius Gallus	IIvir.	4091, 2
Q. Arrasidius	Æd.	2966
C. Arrius	Q	2964
M. Atellius	Q	2964
Attalus, see Claudius.		
Baaso, see Anicius.		
Bassus, see Cominius.		
C. Cæcilius	Æd.	2964
C. Cæsius M.f. IIvir	quinq.	2980
Sex. Cæsius	Æd.	2966
Q. Caleius	Q	2966

- 53 -

Canies, see Saufeius.		
Sex. Capivas	Q (?)	2968
C. Cassius	Q	2966
Celsus, see Mæsius.		
Ti. Claudius Attalus Mamilianus IIvir.		Not. d. Scavi. 1894, p. 96.
M (?), Cominius Bassus	Quinq. Præf.	2964
— Cordus	Q	2964
P. Cornelius	IIvir.	2966
— (Cornelius) Dolabella	IIvir.	2966
— (Corn)elius Rufus	Æd.	2967
L. Curtius	Æd.	2966
— Cur(tius) Sura	IIvir.	2964
M. Decumius	Q (?)	2968
T. Diadumenius (see Antonius Subarus)	IIvir.	4091, 18
C. Dindius	Æd.	2964
Dolabella, see Cornelius. (Also Chap. II, n. 250.)		
— Egnatius	IIvir.	4091,3
Cn. Egnatius	Æd.	2964
L. Fabricius C.f. Vaarus	Æd.	Not. d. Scavi. 1907, p. 137.
C. Feidenatius	Pr.	2999
L. Ferlidius	Q (?)	2968
Fimbria, see Geganius.		
Flaccus, see Saufeius.		
C. Flavius L.f.	IIvir quinq.	2980
Q. Flavius	Q	2966
T. Flavius T.f. Germanus 181 A.D.	Æd. IIvir. IIvir. QQ	2922
— (Fl)avius Musca	Q	2965
Gallus, see Aquilius.		

Sex. Geganius Finbria	IIvir.	4091, 1
Germanus, see Flavius.		
— [I]nstacilius	Æd.	2964
C. Iuc ... Rufus[319]	Q	2964
Lælianus, see Lutatius.		
M'. Later ...[320] (See Add. 4091, 12)	Q	4091, 12
T. Livius	Æd.	2964
T. Long ... Priscus	IIvir.	4091, 4
T. Lucretius	IIvir.	2966
Sex. Lutatius Q.f. Lælianus Oppianicus Petronianu	Pr.	2930
— Macrin(ius) Nerian(us)	Æd.	4091, 10
Sex. Mæsius Sex. f. Celsus	Q. Æd. IIvir.	2989
L. Mag(ulnius) M.f.	Q	4091, 13
C. Magulnius C.f. Scato	Q	2990
C. Magulnius C.f. Scato Maxs(umus)	Pr.	2906
M. Magulnius Sp. f.M.n. Scato.	Pr.(?)	3008
Mamilianus, see Claudius.		
— Manilei Post	A(e)d.	2964
— Mecanius	IIvir.	4091, 5
M. Mersieius C.f.	Æd.	2975
C. Messienus	IIvir.	2966
Q. Mestrius	IIvir.	4091, 6
— — Minus	Quinq.	2964
Musca, see Flavius.		
L. Nassius	Æd.	2966
M. Naut(ius)	Q	4091, 14
Nerianus, see Macrinius.		
C. Ninn(ius)	IIvir.(?)	2968
Oppianicus, see Lutatius.		
L. Orcevius	Pr.	2902

C. Orcivi(us)	Pr. IIvir.	2994
C. Paccius	IIvir. (?)	2968
Paullus, see Acilius.		
L. Petisius Potens	IIvir.	2964
Petronianus, see Lutatius.		
M. Petronius	Quinq.	2966
(M). Petronius Rufus	IIvir.	2964
M. Petronius Rufus	Quinq. Præf.	2964
Planta, see Treb ... ti		
C. Pom pei us	IIvir.	2964
Sex. Pomp(eius)	IIvir. Præf.	2995
Pontanus, see Saufeius.		
Potens, see Petisius.		
Prænestinus prætor (Chap. II, n. 185.) Livy IX, 16, 17.		
Priscus, see Long ...		
Pulcher, see Vettius.		
— Punicus Lig ...	IIvir.	2964
C. Ræcius	IIvir.	2964
M. Ræcius	Q	2964
— Rotanius	Æd	2966
Rufus, see Cornelius, Iuc ..., Petronius, Tertius.		
Rutilus, see Saufeius.		
T. Sabidius Sabinus	IIvir.	Not. d. Scavi. 1894, p. 96.
— — Sabinus	Q	2967
C. Salvius	IIvir.	2966
C. Salvius	IIvir.	2964
M. Samiarius	Q	2966
C. Sa(mi)us	Pr.	2999

— Saufei(us)	Pr. IIvir.	2994
M. Saufe(ius) ... Canies	Aid.	Not. d. Scavi. 1907, p. 137.
C. Saufeius C.f. Flaccus	Pr.	2906
C. Saufeius C.f. Flacus	Q	3002
L. Saufeius C.f. Flaccus	Q	3001
C. Saufeius C.f. Pontanus	Æd.	3000
M. Saufeius L.f. Pontanus	Æd.	3000
M. Saufeius M.f. Rutilus	Q	3002
Scato, see Magulnius.		
P. Scrib(onius)	IIvir.	4091, 3
— — Sedatus	Q. Pr(æf).	2965
Septimus, see Annius.		
C. Sertorius	Q	2966
Q. Spid	Q (?)	2969
— Statiolenus	Q	2966
L. Statius Sal. f.	IIvir.	3013
Subarus, see Antonius.		
C. Tampius C.f. Tarenteinus	Pr.	2890
C. Tappurius	IIvir.	4091, 6
Tarenteinus, see Tampius.		
— Tedusius T. (f.)	IIvir.	3012a
M. Tere ... Cl ...	IIvir.	4091, 7
— Tert(ius) Rufus	IIvir.	2998
C. Thorenas	Q	2964
L. Tondeius L.f.M.n.	Pr. (?)	3008
C. Treb ... Pianta	IIvir.	4091, 4
(Se)x. Truttidius	IIvir.	2964
Vaarus, see Fabricius.		
— (?)cius Valer(ianus)	Q	2967
M. Valerius	Q	2964

Varus, see Voluntilius.	Æd. (?)	2964
— Vassius V.		
L. Vatron(ius)	Pr.	2902
C. Velius	Æd.	2964
Q. Vettius T. (f) Pulcher	IIvir.	3012
C. Vibius	Æd.	2966
Q. Vibuleius L.f.	IIvir.	3013
Cn. Voesius Cn. f. Aper.	Q. Æd. IIvir.	3014
C. Voluntilius Q.f. Varus	IIvir.	3020
— — —	IIvir. IIvir. Quinqu.	4091, 8

CHRONOLOGICAL LIST OF THE MUNICIPAL OFFICERS OF PRÆNESTE.

BEFORE PRÆNESTE WAS A COLONY.

DATE B.C.	IIVIRI	AEDILES	QUÆSTORES.
9	Prænestinus prætor.		
5	M. Anicius.		
{ {		{ M. Anicius L.f. Baaso {M. Mersieius C.f.	
{ { { { {	{C. Samius {C. Feidenatius {C. Tampius C.f. Tarenteinus {C. Vatronius {L. Orcevius		
2{ 8{		{C. Saufeius C.f. Pontanus {M. Saufeius L.f.	
			C. Magulnius C.f. Scato
e{ r{	{L. Tondeius L.f.M.n. {M. Magulnius Sp. f.M.n. Scato		
o{ f{		{L. Fabricius C.f. Varrus {M. Saufe(ius) Canies	

- 58 -

e{
B{

{C. Magulnius C.f. Scato
{ Maxsumus
{C. Saufeius C.f. Flaccus

{

3 {C. Orcivius} Praestores
or {   } isdem
2 (?) {—Saufeius} Duumviri.

{M. Saufeius M.f.
Rutilus
{C. Saufeius C.f. Flacus

{L. Saufeius C.f. Flaccus

A Senate is mentioned in the inscriptions C.I.L., XIV, 2990, 3000, 3001, 3002.

AFTER PRÆNESTE WAS A COLONY.

DATE	IIVIRI	AEDILES	QUÆSTORES.
B.C.			
80-75 (?)			... Sabinus
2d year	{... nus. { [... ter.	{— (Corn)elius Rufus	— (?)cius Valer(ianus)
80-50			
1st year	— (Cornelius) Dolabella	— Rotanius.	{M. Samiarius {Q. (Fl)avius.
2d year	{C. Messienus. {P. Cornelius	{Sex. Cæsius. {L. Nassius.	{Q. Caleius {C. Sertorius.
3d year	{C. Salvius {T. Lucretius	{L. Curtius {C. Vibius	{— Statiolenus. {C. Cassius
4th year	M. Petronius, Quinqu.	Q. Arrasidius.	T. Aponius
75-50			
1st year		.	{M. Decumius. {L. Ferlidius.
2d year	{C. Paccius. {C. Ninn(ius).	{C. Albinius. {Sex. Po..	{Sex. Capivas. {C. M...
?	{C. Cæsius M.f.} Duoviri		

	{C. Flavius L.f. } Quinqu.		
?	{Q. Vettius T. (f.) Pulcher. {— Tedusius T. (f.)		
?	{Q. Vibuleius L.f. {L. Statius Sal. f.		
A.D.			
12			M. Atellius.
13	C. Raecius.	{— (—) lius. {C. Velius.	{— Accius ...us. {M. Valerius.
14	{Germanicus Cæsar Quinqu. {Drusus Cæsar {M. Cominius Bassus Pr. {M. Petronius Rufus	{C. Dindius. {Cn. Egnatius.	{C. Iuc... Rufus {C. Thorenas
15	{Cn. Pom(pei)us. {— Curtius?) Sura.		{M. Ræcius. {— Cordus.
16	{L. Petisius Potens {C. Salvius.	{C. Dindius. {T. Livius.	{L. Aiacius. {C. Arrius.
?		— Vassius	
?	— Punicus.	— Manilei.	
?	... Minus Quinq.	— (?) rius.	
?	(Se)x Truttidi(us).	C. Cæcilius.	
?	(M.) Petronius Rufus.	— (I)nstacilius.	
1st year			— Sedatus.
2d year	... lus		— (Fl)avius Musca.
3d year	{Nero et Drusus } Duoviri {Germanici f. } Quinq. {.... } Præf. {... Sedatus. }		
101	{Ti. Claudius Attalus Mamilianus. {T. Sabidius Sabinus.		
100-256	{P. Annius Septimus. {Sex. Geganius Fimbria.		
	P. Aquilius Gallus.		
250	{— Egnatius. {P. Scrib(onius).		

- 60 -

{T. Long... Prisc(us).
{C. Treb... Planta.
—Mecanius.
{Q. Mestrius.
{C. Tappurius.
M. Tere ... Cl...
C. Voluntilius Q.f. Varus

— Macrin(ius)
Nerian(us).

M'. Later...
L. Mag(ulnius) M.f.

{(M). Antonius Subarus.   M. Naut(ius).
{T. Diadumenius.

Decuriones populusque colonia Prænestin., C.I.L., XIV, 2898, 2899; decuriones populusque 2970, 2971, Not. d. Scavi 1894, P. 96; other mention of decuriones 2980, 2987, 2992, 3013; ordo populusque 2914; decretum ordinis 2991; curiales, in the late empire, Symmachus, Rel., 28, 4.

NOTES:

[1]

Strabo V, 3, II.

[2]

We know that in 380 B.C. Præneste had eight towns under her jurisdiction, and that they must have been relatively near by. Livy VI, 29, 6: octo præterea oppida erant sub dicione Prænestinorum. Festus, p. 550 (de Ponor): T. Quintius Dictator cum per novem dies totidem urbes et decimam Præneste cepisset, and the story of the golden crown offered to Jupiter as the result of this rapid campaign, and the statue which was carried away from Præneste (Livy VI, 29, 8), all show that the domain of Præneste was both of extent and of consequence.

[3]

Nibby, Analisi, II, p. 475.

[4]

Cecconi, Storia di Palestrina, p. 11, n. 74.

[5]

Cecconi, Storia di Palestrina, p. 227 ff.; Marucchi, Guida Archeologica, p. 14; Nibby, Analisi, p. 483; Volpi, Latium vetus de Præn., chap 2; Tomassetti, Della Campagna Romana, p. 167.

[6]

Cecconi, Storia di Palestrina, p. 11.

[7]

Nibby, Analisi, II, p. 484 from Muratori, Rerum Italicarum Scriptores, III, i, p. 301.

[8]

Cecconi, Storia di Palestrina, p. 402.

[9]

Cecconi, Storia di Palestrina, p. 277, n. 36, from Epist., 474: Bonifacius VIII concedit Episcopo Civitatis Papalis Locum, ubi fuerunt olim Civitas Prænestina, eiusque Castrum, quod dicebatur Mons, et Rocca; ac etiam Civitas Papalis postmodum destructa, cum Territorio et Turri de Marmoribus, et Valle Gloriæ; nec non Castrum Novum Tiburtinum 2 Id. April. an. VI; Petrini, Memorie Prenestine, p. 136; Civitas prædicta cum Rocca, et Monte, cum Territorio ipsius posita est in districtu Urbis in contrata, quæ dicitur Romangia.

[10]

Ashby, Papers of the British School at Rome, Vol. I, p. 213, and Maps IV and VI. Cecconi, Storia di Palestrina, p. 19, n. 34.

[11]

Livy VIII, 12, 7: Pedanos tuebatur Tiburs, Prænestinus Veliternusque populus, etc. Livy VII, 12, 8: quod Gallos mox Præneste venisse atque inde circa Pedum consedisse auditum est. Livy II, 39, 4; Dion. Hal. VIII, 19, 3; Horace, Epist, I, 4, 2. Cluverius, p. 966, thinks Pedum is Gallicano, as does Nibby with very good reason, Analisi, II, p. 552, and Tomassetti, Della Campagna Romana, p. 176. Ashby, Classical Topography of the Roman Campagna in Papers of the British School at Rome, I, p. 205, thinks Pedum can not be located with certainty, but rather inclines to Zagarolo.

[12]

There are some good ancient tufa quarries too on the southern slope of Colle S. Rocco, to which a branch road from Præneste ran. Fernique, Étude sur Préneste, p. 104.

[13]

C.I.L., XIV, 2940 found at S. Pastore.

[14]

Now the Maremmana inferiore, Ashby, Classical Topog. of the Roman Campagna, I, pp. 205, 267.

[15]

Ashby, Classical Topog. of the Roman Campagna, I, p. 206, finds on the Colle del Pero an ampitheatre and a great many remains of imperial times, but considers it the probable site of an early village.

[16]

Fernique, Étude sur Préneste, p. 120, wishes to connect Marcigliano and Ceciliano with the gentes Marcia and Cæcilia, but it is impossible to do more than guess, and the rather few names of these gentes at Præneste make the guess improbable. It is also impossible to locate regio Cæsariana mentioned as a possession of Præneste by Symmachus, Rel., XXVIII, 4, in the year 384 A.D. Eutropius II, 12 gets some confirmation of his argument from the modern name Campo di Pirro which still clings to the ridge west of Præneste.

[17]

The author himself saw all the excavations here along the road during the year 1907, of which there is a full account in the Not. d. Scavi, Ser. 5, 4 (1907), p. 19. Excavations began on these tombs in 1738, and have been carried on spasmodically ever since. There were excavations again in 1825 (Marucchi, Guida Archeologica, p. 21), but it was in 1855 that the more extensive excavations were made which caused so much stir among archæologists (Marucchi, l.c., p. 21, notes 1-7). For the excavations see Bull. dell'Instituto. 1858, p. 93 ff., 1866, p. 133, 1869, p. 164, 1870, p. 97, 1883, p. 12; Not. d. Scavi, 2 (1877-78), pp. 101, 157, 390, 10 (1882-83), p. 584; Revue Arch., XXXV (1878), p. 234; Plan of necropolis in Garucci, Dissertazioni Arch., plate XII. Again in 1862 there were excavations of importance made in the Vigna Velluti, to the right of the road to Marcigliano. It was thought that the exact boundaries of the necropolis on the north and south had been found because of the little columns of peperino 41 inches high by 8-8/10 inches square, which were in situ, and seemed to serve no other purpose than that of sepulchral cippi or boundary stones. Garucci, Dissertazioni Arch., I, p. 148; Archæologia, 41 (1867), p. 190.

[18]

C.I.L., XIV, 2987.

[19]

The papal documents read sometimes in Latin, territorium Prænestinum or Civitas Prænestina, but often the town itself is mentioned in its changing nomenclature, Pellestrina, Pinestrino, Penestre (Cecconi, Storia di Palestrina, p. II; Nibby, Analisi, II, pp. 475, 483).

[20]

There is nothing to show that Poli ever belonged in any way to ancient Præneste.

[21]

Rather a variety of cappellaccio, according to my own observations. See Not. d. Scavi, Ser. 5, 5 (1897), p. 259.

[22]

The temple in Cave is of the same tufa (Fernique, Étude sur Préneste, p. 104). The quarries down toward Gallicano supplied tufa of the same texture, but the quarries are too small to have supplied much. But this tufa from the ridge back of the town seems not to have been used in Gallicano to any great extent, for the tufa there is of a different kind and comes from the different cuts in the ridges on either side of the town, and from a quarry just west of the town across the valley.

[23]

Plautus, Truc., 691 (see [Probus] de ultimis syllabis, p. 263, 8 (Keil); C.I.L., XIV, p. 288, n. 9); Plautus, Trin., 609 (Festus, p. 544 (de Ponor), Mommsen, Abhand. d. berl. Akad., 1864, p. 70); Quintilian I, 5, 56; Festus under "tongere," p. 539 (de Ponor), and under "nefrendes," p. 161 (de Ponor).

[24]

Cave has been attached rather more to Genazzano during Papal rule than to Præneste, and it belongs to the electoral college of Subiaco, Tomassetti, Delia Campagna Romana, p. 182.

[25]

I heard everywhere bitter and slighting remarks in Præneste about Cave, and much fun made of the Cave dialect. When there are church festivals at Cave the women usually go, but the men not often, for the facts bear out the tradition that there is usually a fight. Tomassetti, Della Campagna Romana, p. 183, remarks upon the differences in dialect.

[26]

Mommsen, Bull. dell'Instituto, 1862, p. 38, thinks that the civilization in Præneste was far ahead of that of the other Latin cities.

[27]

It is to be noted that this Marcigliana road was not to tap the trade route along the Volscian side of the Liris-Trerus valley, which ran under Artena and through Valmontone. It did not reach so far. It was meant rather as a threat to that route.

[28]

Whether these towns are Pedum or Bola, Scaptia, and Querquetula is not a question here at all.

[29]

Gatti, in Not. d. Scavi, 1903, p. 576, in connection with the Arlenius inscription, found on the site of the new Forum below Præneste in 1903, which mentions Ad Duas Casas as confinium territorio Præstinæ, thought that it was possible to identify this place with a fundus and possessio Duas Casas below Tibur under Monte Gennaro, and thus to extend the domain of Præneste that far, but as Huelsen saw (Mitth. des k.d. Arch, Inst., 19 (1904), p. 150), that is manifestly impossible, doubly so from the modern analogies which he quotes (l.c., note 2) from the Dizionario dei Comuni d'Italia.

[30]

It might be objected that because Pietro Colonna in 1092 A.D. assaulted and took Cave as his first step in his revolt against Clement III (Cecconi, Storia di Palestrina, p. 240), that Cave was at that time a dependency of Præneste. But it has been shown that Præneste's diocesan territory expanded and shrunk very much at different times, and that in general the extent of a diocese, when larger, depends on principles which ancient topography will not allow. And too it can as well be said that

Pietro Colonna was paying up ancient grudge against Cave, and certainly also he realized that of all the towns near Præneste, Cave was strategically the best from which to attack, and this most certainly shows that in ancient times such natural barriers between the two must have been practically impassable.

[31] To be more exact, on the least precipitous side, that which looks directly toward Rocca di Cave.

[32] To anticipate any one saying that this scarping is modern, and was done to make the approach to the Via del Colonnaro, I will say that the modern part of it is insignificant, and can be most plainly distinguished, and further, that the two pieces of opus incertum which are there, as shown also in Fernique's map, Étude sur Préneste, opp. p. 222, are Sullan in date.

[33] Fernique, Étude sur Préneste, map facing p. 222. His book is on the whole the best one on Præneste but leaves much to be desired when the question is one of topography or epigraphy (see Dessau's comment C.I.L., XIV, p. 294, n. 4). Even Marucchi, Guida Arch., p. 68, n. 1, took the word of a citizen of the town who wrote him that parts of a wall of opus quadratum could be traced along the Via dello Spregato, and so fell into error. Blondel, Mélanges d'archéologie et d'histoire de l'école française de Rome, 1882, plate 5, shows a little of this polygonal cyclopean construction.

[34] Nibby, Analisi, II, p. 511, wrote his note on the wall beyond San Francesco from memory. He says that one follows the monastery wall down, and then comes to a big reservoir. The monastery wall has only a few stones from the cyclopean wall in it, and they are set in among rubble, and are plainly a few pieces from the upper wall above the gate. The reservoir which he reaches is half a mile away across a depression several hundred feet deep, and there is no possible connection, for the reservoir is over on Colle San Martino, not on the hill of Præneste at all.

[35]

The postern or portella is just what one would expect near a corner of the wall, as a less important and smaller entrance to a terrace less wide than the main one above it, which had its big gates at west and east, the Porta San Francesco and the Porta del Cappuccini. The Porta San Francesco is proved old and famous by C.I.L., XIV, 3343, where supra viam is all that is necessary to designate the road from this gate. Again an antica via in Via dello Spregato (Not. d. Scavi, I (1885), p. 139, shows that inside this oldest cross wall there was a road part way along it, at least.)

[36]

The Cyclopean wall inside the Porta del Sole was laid bare in 1890, Not. d. Scavi, 7-8 (1890), p. 38.

[37]

Nibby, Analisi, II, p. 501: "A destra della contrada degli Arconi due cippi simili a quelli del pomerio di Roma furono scoperti nel risarcire la strada l'anno 1824."

[38]

Some of the paving stones are still to be seen in situ under the modern wall which runs up from the brick reservoir of imperial date. This wall was to sustain the refuse which was thrown over the city wall. The place between the walls is now a garden.

[39]

I have examined with care every foot of the present western wall on which the houses are built, from the outside, and from the cellars inside, and find no traces of antiquity, except the few stones here and there set in late rubble in such a way that it is sure they have been simply picked up somewhere and brought there for use as extra material.

[40]

C.I.L., XIV., 3029; PED XXC. Nibby, Analisi, II, p. 497, mentions an inscription, certainly this one, but reads it PED XXX, and says it is in letters of the most ancient form. This is not true. The letters are not so very ancient. I was led by his note to examine every stone in the cyclopean wall around the whole city, but no further inscription was forthcoming.

[41]

This stretch of opus incertum is Sullan reconstruction when he made a western approach to the Porta Triumphalis to correspond to the one at the east on the arches. This piece of wall is strongly made, and is exactly like a piece of opus incertum wall near the Stabian gate at Pompeii, which Professor Man told me was undoubtedly Sullan.

[42]

Marucchi, Guida Arch., p. 19, who is usually a good authority on Præneste, thinks that all the opus quadratum walls were built as surrounding walls for the great sanctuary of Fortuna. But the facts will not bear out his theory. Ovid, Fasti VI, 61-62, III, 92; Preller, Roem. Myth., 2, 191, are interesting in this connection.

[43]

I could get no exact measurements of the reservoir, for the water was about knee deep, and I was unable to persuade my guides to venture far from the entrance, but I carried a candle to the walls on both sides and one end.

[44]

At some places the concrete was poured in behind the wall between it and the shelving cliff, at other places it is built up like the wall. The marks of the stones in the concrete can be seen most plainly near Porta S. Martino (Fernique, Étude sur Préneste, p. 104, also mentions it). The same thing is true at various places all along the wall.

[45]

Fernique, Étude sur Préneste, p. 107, has exact measurements of the walls.

[46]

Fernique, Étude sur Préneste, p. 108, from Cecconi, Storia di Palestrina, p. 43, considers as a possibility a road from each side,

[47]

but he is trying only to make an approach to the temple with corresponding parts, and besides he advances no proofs.

There seems to have been only a postern in the ancient wall inside the present Porta del Sole.

[48]

Many feet of this ancient pavement were laid bare during the excavations in April, 1907, which I myself saw, and illustrations of which are published in the Notizie d. Scavi, Ser. 5, 4 (1907), pp. 136, 292.

[49]

Marucchi, Guida Arch., p. 57 ff. for argument and proof, beginning with Varro, de l. l. VI, 4: ut Præneste incisum in solario vidi.

[50]

Cecconi, Storia di Palestrina, p. 43.

[51]

The continuation of the slope is the same, and the method of making roads in the serpentine style to reach a gate leading to the important part of town, is not only the common method employed for hill towns, but the natural and necessary one, not only in ancient times, but still today.

[52]

Through the courtesy of the Mayor and the Municipal Secretary of Palestrina, I had the only exact map in existence of modern Palestrina to work with. This map was getting in bad condition, so I traced it, and had photographic copies made of it, and presented a mounted copy to the city. This map shows these wall alignments and the changes in direction of the cyclopean wall on the east of the city. Fernique seems to have drawn offhand from this map, so his plan (l.c., facing p. 222) is rather carelessly done.

I shall publish the map in completeness within a few years, in a place where the epochs of the growth of the city can be shown in colors.

[53]

I called the attention of Dr. Esther B. Van Deman, Carnegie Fellow in the American School of Classical Studies in Rome, who came out to Palestrina, and kindly went over many of my results with me, to this piece of wall, and she agreed with me that it had been an approach to the terrace in ancient times.

[54]

C.I.L., XIV, 2850. The inscription was on a small cippus, and was seen in a great many different places, so no argument can be drawn from its provenience.

[55]

This may have been the base for the statue of M. Anicius, so famous after his defense at Casilinum. Livy XXIII, 19, 17-18.

It might not be a bad guess to say that the Porta Triumphalis first got its name when M. Anicius returned with his proud cohort to Præneste.

[56]

Not. d. Scavi, 7-8 (1890), p. 38. This platform is a little over three feet above the level of the modern piazza, but is now hidden under the steps to the Corso. But the piece of restraining wall is still to be seen in the piazza, and it is of the same style of opus quadratum construction as the walls below the Barberini gardens.

[57]

Strabo V, 3, II (238, 10): ερυμνη μεν ουν εκατερα, πολυ δ'ερυμνοτεραερυμνοτε Πραινεστος.

[58]

Plutarch, Sulla, XXVIII: Μαριος δε φευγων εις Πραινεστον ηδη τας πυλας ευρε κεκλειμενας.

[59]

[60]
    Cecconi, Storia di Palestrina, p. 282; Nibby, Analisi, II, p. 491.

[61]
    Petrini, Memorie Prenestine, pp. 180-181. The walls were built in muro merlato. It is not certain where the Murozzo and Truglio were. Petrini guesses at their site on grounds of derivation.

[62]
    Petrini, Memorie Prenestine, p. 248.

[63]
    Also called Porta S. Giacomo, or dell'Ospedale.

[64]
    Petrini, Memorie Prenestine, p. 252.

[65]
    Closed seemingly in Sullan times.

[66]
    The rude corbeling of one side of the gate is still very plainly to be seen. The gate is filled with mediæval stone work.

[67]
    There is a wooden gate here, which can be opened, but it only leads out upon a garden and a dumping ground above a cliff.

[68]
    This was the only means of getting out to the little stream that ran down the depression shown in plate III, and over to the hill of S. Martino, which with the slope east of the city could properly be called Monte Glicestro outside the walls.

    This gate is now a mediæval tower gate, but the stones of the cyclopean wall are still in situ, and show three stones, with straight edge, one above the other, on each side of the present gate, and the wall here has a jog of twenty feet. The road out this gate could not be seen except from down on the Cave road, and it gave an outlet to some springs under the citadel, and to the valley back toward Capranica.

[69]

This last stretch of the wall did not follow the present wall, but ran up directly back of S. Maria del'Carmine, and was on the east side of the rough and steep track which borders the eastern side of the present Franciscan monastery.

[70]

The several courses of opus quadratum which were found a few years ago, and are at the east entrance to the Corso built into the wall of a lumber store, are continued also inside that wall, and seem to be the remains of a gate tower.

[71]

See page 28. This gap in the wall is still another proof for the gate, for it was down the road, which was paved, that the water ran after rainstorms, if at no other time.

[72]

This gate is very prettily named by Cecconi, Spiegazione de Numeri, Map facing page 1: l'antica Porta di San Martino chiusa.

[73]

Since the excavations of the past two years, nothing has been written to show what relations a few newly discovered pieces of ancient paved roads have to the city and to its gates, and for that reason it becomes necessary to say something about a matter only tolerably treated by the writers on Præneste up to their dates of publication.

[74]

Ashby, Classical Topog. of the Roman Campagna, in Papers of the British School at Rome, Vol. 1, Map VI.

[75]

This road is proved as ancient by the discovery in 1906 (Not. d. Scavi, Ser. 5, 3 (1906), p. 317) of a small paved road, a diverticolo, in front of the church of S. Lucia, which is a direct continuation of the Via degli Arconi. This diverticolo ran out the Colle dell'Oro. See Cecconi, Storia di Palestrina, p. 20, n. 37; Fernique, Étude sur Préneste, p. 122; Marucchi, Guida Archeologica, p. 122.

[76]

This road to Marcigliano had nothing to do with either the Præenestina or the Labicana. Not. d. Scavi, Ser. 5, 5 (1897), p. 255; 2 (1877-78), p. 157; Bull. dell'Inst., 1876, pp. 117 ff. make the via S. Maria the eastern boundary of the necropolis.

[77]

Not. d. Scavi, 11 (1903), pp. 23-25.

[78]

Probably the store room of some little shop which sold the exvotos. Bull. dell'Inst., 1883, p. 28.

[79]

Bull. dell'Inst., 1871, p. 72 for tombs found on both sides the modern road to Rome, the exact provenience being the vocabolo S. Rocco, on the Frattini place; Stevenson, Bull. dell'Inst., 1883, pp. 12 ff., for tombs in the vigna Soleti along the diverticolo from the Via Præenestina. Also at Bocce Rodi, one mile west of the city, tombs of the imperial age were found (Not. d. Scavi, 10 (1882-83), p. 600); C.I.L., XIV, 2952, 2991, 4091, 65; Bull. dell'Inst., 1870, p. 98.

[80]

The roads are the present Via Præenestina toward Gallicano, and the Via Præenestina Nuova which crosses the Casilina to join the Labicana. This great deposit of terra cottas was found in 1877 at a depth of twelve feet below the present ground level. Fernique, Revue Arch., XXXV (1878), p. 240, notes 1, 2, and 3, comes to the best conclusions on this find. It was a factory or kiln for the terra cottas, and there was a store in connection at or near the junction of the roads. Other stores of deposits of the same kinds of objects have been found (see Fernique, l.c.) at Falterona, Gabii, Capua, Vicarello; also at the temple of Diana Nemorensis (Bull. dell'Inst., 1871, p. 71), and outside Porta S.

Lorenzo at Rome (Bull. Com., 1876, p. 225), and near Civita Castellana (Bull. dell'Inst., 1880, p. 108).

[81]

Strabo V, 3, 11 (C. 239); ... διωρυξι κρυπταις--πανταχοτεν μεχρι των πεδιων ταις μεν υδρειας χαριν κτλ. ; Vell. Paterc. II, 27, 4.

[82]

As one goes out the Porta S. Francesco and across the depression by the road which winds round to the citadel, he finds both above and below the road several reservoirs hollowed out in the rock of the mountain, which were filled by the rain water which fell above them and ran into them.

[83]

Cola di Rienzo did this (see note 59), and so discovered the method by which the Praenestines communicated with the outside world. Sulla fixed his camp on le Tende, west of the city, that he might have a safe position himself, and yet threaten Praeneste from the rear, from over Colle S. Martino, as well as by an attack in front.

[84]

C.I.L., XIV, 3013, 3014 add., 2978, 2979, 3015.

[85]

Nibby, Analisi, p. 510. It could be seen in 1907, but not so very clearly.

[86]

Cecconi, Storia di Palestrina, p. 79, thinks this reservoir was for storing water for a circus in the valley below. This is most improbable. It was a reservoir to supply a villa which covered the lower part of the slope, as the different remains certainly show.

[87]

Cecconi, Storia di Palestrina, p. 301, n. 30, 31, from Annali int. rerum Italic, scriptorum, Vol. 24, p. 1115; Vol. 21, p. 146, and from Ciacconi, in Eugen. IV, Platina et Blondus.

[88]

The mediæval Italian towns everywhere made use of the Roman aqueducts, and we have from the middle ages practically nothing but repairs on aqueducts, hardly any aqueducts themselves.

[89]

Cecconi, Storia di Palestrina, p. 338, speaks of this aqueduct as "quel mirabile antico cuniculo."

[90]

The springs Acqua Maggiore, Acqua della Nocchia, Acqua del Sambuco, Acqua Ritrovata, Acqua della Formetta (Petrini, Memorie Prenestine, p. 286).

[91]

Fernique, Étude sur Préneste, p. 96 ff., p. 122 ff.; Nibby, Analisi, II, p. 501 ff.; Marucchi, Guida Arch., p. 45.

[92]

Nibby, Analisi, II, p. 503, the sanest of all the writers on Præneste, even made some ruins which he found under the Fiumara house on the east side of town, into the remains of a reservoir to correspond to the one in the Barberini gardens. The structures according to material differ in date about two hundred years.

[93]

C.I.L., XIV, 2911, was found near this reservoir, and Nibby from this, and a likeness to the construction of the Castra Prætoria at Rome, dates it so (Analisi, p. 503).

[94]

This is the opinion of Dr. Esther B. Van Deman of the American School in Rome.

[95]

See above, page 29.

[96]

There is still another small reservoir on the next terrace higher, the so-called Borgo terrace, but I was not able to examine it satisfactorily enough to come to any conclusion. Palestrina is a labyrinth of underground passages. I have explored dozens of them, but the most of them are pockets, and were store rooms or hiding places belonging to the houses under which they were.

[97]

This is shown by the network of drains all through the plain below the city. Strabo V, 3, 11 (C. 239); Vell. Paterc. II, 27, 4; Valer. Max. VI, 8, 2; Cecconi, Storia di Palestrina, p. 77; Fernique, Étude sur Préneste, p. 123.

[98]

Cicero, de Div., II, 41, 85.

[99]

There are many references to the temple. Suetonius, Dom., 15, Tib., 63; Ælius Lampridius, Life of Alex. Severus, XVIII, 4, 6 (Peter); Strabo V, 3, 11 (238, 10); Cicero, de Div., II, 41, 86-87; Plutarch, de fort. Rom. (Moralia, p. 396, 37); C.I.L., I, p. 267; Preller, Roem. Myth. II, 192, 3 (pp. 561-563); Cecconi, Storia di Palestrina, p. 275, n. 29, p. 278, n. 37.

[100]

"La città attuale è intieramente fondata sulle rovine del magnifico tempio della Fortuna," Nibby, Analisi, II, p. 494. "E niuno ignora che il colossale edificio era addossato al declivio del monte prenestino e occupava quasi tutta l'area ove oggi si estende la moderna città," Marucchi, Bull. Com., 32 (1904), p. 233.

[101]

This upper temple is the one mentioned in a manifesto of 1299 A.D. made by the Colonna against the Caetani (Cecconi, Storia di Palestrina, p. 275, n. 29). It is an order of Pope Boniface VIII, ex Codic. Archiv. Castri S. Angeli signat, n. 47, pag. 49: Item, dicunt civitatem Prenestinam cum palatiis nobilissimis et cum templo magno et sollempni ... et cum muris antiquis opere sarracenico factis de lapidibus quadris et magnis totaliter suppositam fuisse exterminio et ruine per ipsum Dominum Bonifacium, etc. Petrini, Memorie Prenestine, p. 419 ff.

Also as to the shape of the upper temple and the number of steps to it, we have certain facts from a document from the archives of the Vatican, published in Petrini, l.c., p. 429; palacii nobilissimi et antiquissimi scalæ de nobilissimo marmore per quas etiam equitando ascendi poterat in Palacium ... quæquidem scalæ erant ultra centum numero. Palacium autem Cæsaris ædificatum ad modum unius C propter primam litteram nominis sui, et templum palatio inhærens, opere sumptuosissimo et nobilissimo ædificatum ad modum s. Mariæ rotundæ de urbe.

[102]

Delbrueck, Hellenistische Bauten in Latium, under Das Heiligtum der Fortuna in Præneste, p. 47 ff.

[103]

Cicero, De Div., II, 41, 85.

[104]

Marucchi wishes to make the east cave the older and the real cave of the sortes. However, he does not know the two best arguments for his case; Lampridius, Alex. Severus, XVIII, 4, 6 (Peter); Huic sors in templo Prænestinæ talis extitit, and Suetonius Tib., 63: non repperisset in arca nisi relata rursus ad templum. Topography is all with the cave on the west, Marucchi is wrong, although he makes a very good case (Bull. Com., 32 (1904), p. 239).

[105]

Cicero, de Div., II, 41, 85: is est hodie locus sæptus religiose propter Iovis pueri, qui lactens cum Iunone Fortunæ in gremio sedens, ... eodemque tempore in eo loco, ubi Fortunæ nunc est ædes, etc.

[106]

C.I.L., XIV, 2867: ...ut Triviam in Iunonario, ut in pronao ædis statuam, etc., and Livy, XXIII, 19, 18 of 216 B.C.: Idem titulus (a laudatory inscription to M. Anicius) tribus signis in æde Fortunæ positis fuit subiectus.

[107]

This question is not topographical and can not be discussed at any length here. But the best solution seems to be that Fortuna as child of Jupiter (Diovo filea primocenia, C.I.L., XIV., 2863, Iovis puer primigenia, C.I.L., XIV, 2862, 2863) was confounded with her name Iovis puer, and another cult tradition which made Fortuna mother of two children. As the Roman deity Jupiter grew in importance, the tendency was for the Romans to misunderstand Iovis puer as the boy god Jupiter, as they really did (Wissowa, Relig. u. Kult. d. Roemer, p. 209), and the pride of the Præstines then made Fortuna the mother of Jupiter and Juno, and considered Primigenia to mean "first born," not "first born of Jupiter."

[108]

The establishment of the present Cathedral of S. Agapito as the basilica of ancient Præneste is due to the acumen of Marucchi, who has made it certain in his writings on the subject. Bull. dell' Inst., 1881, p. 248 ff., 1882, p. 244 ff.; Guida Archeologica, 1885, p. 47 ff.; Bull. Com., 1895, p. 26 ff., 1904, p. 233 ff.

[109]

There are 16 descriptions and plans of the temple. A full bibliography of them is in Delbrueck, Hellenistische Bauten in Latium, pp. 51-52.

[110]

Marucchi. Bull. Com., XXXII (1904), p. 240. I also saw it very plainly by the light of a torch on a pole, when studying the temple in April, 1907.

[111]

See also Revue Arch., XXXIX (1901), p. 469, n. 188.

[112]

C.I.L, XIV, 2864.

[113]

See Henzen, Bull. dell'Inst., 1859, p. 23, from Paulus ex Festo under manceps. This claims that probably the manceps was in charge of the maintenance (manutenzione) of the temple, and the cellarii of the cella proper, because ædituí, of whom we have no mention, are the proper custodians of the entire temple, precinct and all.

[114]

C.I.L., XIV, 3007. See Jordan, Topog. d. Stadt Rom, I, 2, p. 365, n. 73.

[115]

See Delbrueck, l.c., p. 62.

[116]

C.I.L., XIV, 2922; also on bricks, Ann. dell'Inst., 1855, p. 86—C.I.L., XIV, 4091, 9.

[117]

C.I.L., XIV, 2980; C. Cæsius M.f.C. Flavius L.f. Duovir Quinq. ædem et portic d.d. fac. coer. eidemq. prob.

[118]

C.I.L., XIV, 2995; ...summa porticum mar[moribus]—albario adiecta. Dessau says on "some public building," which is too easy. See Vitruvius, De Architectura, 7, 2; Pliny, XXXVI, 177.

[119]

Petrini, Memorie Prenestine, p. 430. See also Juvenal XIV, 88; Friedlænder, Sittengeschichte Roms, II, 107, 10.

[120]

Delbrueck, l.c., p. 62, with illustration.

[121]

Although Suaresius (Thesaurus Antiq. Italiæ, VIII, Part IV, plate, p. 38) uses some worthless inscriptions in making such a point, his idea is good. Perhaps the lettered blocks drawn for the inquirer from the arca were arranged here on this slab. Another possibility is that it was a place of record of noted cures or answers of the Goddess. Such inscriptions are well known from the temple of Æsculapius at Epidaurus, Cavvadias, Εφημ Αρχ. , 1883, p. 1975; Michel, Recueil d'insc. grec., 1069 ff.

[122]

Mommsen, Unterital. Dialekte, pp. 320, 324; Marquardt, Staatsverwaltung, 3, p. 271, n. 8. See Marucchi, Bull. Com., 32 (1904), p. 10.

[123]

Delbrueck, l.c., pp. 50, 59, does prove that there is no reason why λιθοστρωτον can not mean a mosaic floor of colored marble, but he forgets comparisons with the date of other Roman mosaics, and that Pliny would not have missed the opportunity of describing such wonderful mosaics as the two in Præneste. Marucchi, Bull. Com., 32 (1904), p. 251 goes far afield in his Isityches (Isis-Fortuna) quest, and gets no results.

The latest discussion of the subject was a joint debate held under the auspices of the Associazione Archeologica di Palestrina between Professors Marucchi and Vaglieri, which is published thus far only in the daily papers, the Corriere D'Italia of Oct. 2, 1907, and taken up in an article by Attilio Rossi in La Tribuna of October 11, 1907. Vaglieri, in the newspaper article quoted, holds that the mosaic is the work of Claudius Ælianus, who lived in the latter half of the second century A.D. Marucchi, in the same place, says that in the porticoes of the upper temple are traces of mosaic which he attributes to the gift of Sulla mentioned by Pliny XXXVI, 189, but in urging this he must shift delubrum Fortunæ to the Cortina terrace and that is entirely impossible.

I may say that a careful study and a long paper on the Barberini mosaic has just been written by Cav. Francesco Coltellacci, Segretario Comunale di Palestrina, which I had the privilege of reading in manuscript.

[124]

For the many opinions as to the subject of the mosaic, see Marucchi, Guida Arch., p. 75.

[125]

This has been supposed to be a villa of Hadrian's because the Braschi Antinoüs was found here, and because we find bricks in the walls with stamps which date from Hadrian's time. But the best proof that this building, which is under the modern cemetery, is Hadrian's, is that the measurements of the walls are the same as those in his villa below Tibur. Dr. Van Deman, of the American School in Rome, spent two days with me in going over this building and comparing measurements with the villa at Tibur. I shall publish a plan of the villa in the near future. See Fernique, Étude sur Préneste, p. 120, for a meagre description of the villa.

[126]

Delbrueck, l.c., p. 58, n. 1.

[127]

The ærarium is under the temple and at the same time cut back into the solid rock of the cliff just across the road at one corner of the basilica. An ærarium at Rome under the temple of Saturn is always mentioned in this connection. There is also a chamber of the same sort at the upper end of the shops in front of the basilica Æmilia in the Roman Forum, to which Boni has given the name "carcere," but Huelsen thinks rightly that it is a treasury of some sort. There is a like treasury in Pompeii back of the market, so Mau thinks, Vaglieri in Corriere D'Italia, Oct 2, 1907.

[128]

See note 106.

[129]

C.I.L., XIV, 2875. This dedication of "coques atriensis" probably belongs to the upper temple.

[130]

Alle Quadrelle casale verso Cave e Valmontone, Cecconi, Storia di Palestrina, p. 70; Chaupy, Maison d'Horace, II, p. 317; Petrini, Memorie Prenestine, p. 326, n. 9.

[131]

The martyr suffered death contra civitatem præenestinam ubi sunt duæ viæ, Marucchi, Guida Arch., p. 144, n. 3, from Martirol. Adonis, 18 Aug. Cod. Vat. Regin., n. 511 (11th cent. A.D.).

[132]

C.I.L., XIV, 3014; Bull. munic., 2 (1874), p. 86; C.I.L., VI, p. 885, n. 1744a; Tac. Ann., XV, 46 (65 A.D.); Friedlænder, Sittengeschichte Roms, II, p. 377; Cicero, pro Plancio, XXVI, 63; Epist. ad Att., XII, 2, 2; Cassiodorus, Variæ, VI, 15.

[133]

A black and white mosaic of late pattern was found there during the excavations. Not. d. Scavi, 1877, p. 328; Fernique, Revue Arch., XXXV (1878), p. 233; Fronto, p. 157 (Naber).

[134]

On Le Colonelle toward S. Pastore. Cecconi, Storia di Palestrina, p. 60.

[135]

I think this better than the supposition that these libraries were put up by a man skilled in public and private law. See C.I.L, XIV, 2916.

[136]

Not d. Scavi, Ser. 5, 4 (1896), p. 330.

[137]

Livy XXIII, 19, 17-18: statua cius (M. Anicii) indicio fuit, Præneste in foro statuta, loricata, amicta toga, velato capite, etc.

[138]

See also the drawing and illustrations, one of which, no. 2, is from a photograph of mine, in Not. d. Scavi, 1907, pp. 290-292. The basilica is built in old opus quadratum of tufa, Not. d. Scavi, I (1885), p. 256.

[139]

In April, 1882 (Not. d. Scavi, 10 (1882-83), p. 418), during a reconstruction of the cathedral of S. Agapito, ancient pavement was found in a street back of the cathedral, and many pieces of Doric columns which must have been from the peristile of the basilica. See Plate IV for new pieces just found of these Doric columns.

[140]

Not. d. Scavi, Ser. 5, 4 (1896), p. 49. Also in same place: "l'area sacra adiacente al celebre santuario della Fortuna Primigenia" is the description of the cortile of the Seminary.

[141]

More discussion of this point above in connection with the temple, page 51.

[142]

I was in Præneste during all the excavations of 1907, and made these photographs while I was there.

[143]

The drawing of the Not. d. Scavi, 1907, p. 290, which shows a probable portico is not exact.

[144]

It is now called the Via delle Scalette.

[145]

Delbrueck, Hellenistische Bauten in Latium, p. 58.

[146]

See full-page illustration in Delbrueck, l.c., p. 79.

[147]

See page 30. But ex d(ecreto) d(ecurionum) would refer better to the Sullan forum below the town, especially as the two bases set up to Pax Augusti and Securitas Augusti (C.I.L., XIV, 2898, 2899) were found down on the site of the lower forum.

[148]

[148]

    C.I.L., XIV, 2908, 2919, 2916, 2937, 2946, 3314, 3340.

[149]

    C.I.L., XIV, 2917, 2919, 2922, 2924, 2929, 2934, 2955, 2997, 3014, Not. d. Scavi, 1903, p. 576.

[150]

    F. Barnabei, Not. d. Scavi, 1894, p. 96.

[151]

    C.I.L., XIV, 2914.

[152]

    Not. d. Scavi, 1897, p. 421; 1904, p. 393.

[153]

    Foggini, Fast. anni romani, 1774, preface, and Mommsen, C.I.L., I, p. 311 (from Acta acad. Berol., 1864, p. 235; See also Henzen, Bull. dell'Inst., 1864, p. 70), were both wrong in putting the new forum out at le quadrelle, because a number of fragments of the calendar of Verrius Flaccus were found there. Marucchi proves this in his Guida Arch., p. 100, Nuovo Bull. d'Arch. crist., 1899, pp. 229-230; Bull. Com., XXXII (1904), p. 276.

    The passage from Suetonius, De Gram., 17 (vita M. Verri Flacci), is always to be cited as proof of the forum, and that it had a well-marked upper and lower portion; Statuam habet (M. Verrius Flaccus) Præneste in superiore fori parte circa hemicyclium, in quo fastos a se ordinatos et marmoreo parieti incisos publicarat.

[154]

    Delbrueck, Hellenistische Bauten in Latium, p. 50, n. 1, from Preller, Roemische Mythologie, II, p. 191, n. 1.

[155]

    C.I.L., XIV, 4097, 4105a, 4106f.

[156]

Petrini, Memorie Prenestine, p. 320, n. 19.

[157]

Cecconi, Storia di Palestrina, p. 35.

[158]

Tibur shows 1 to 32 and Præneste 1 to 49 names of inhabitants from the Umbro-Sabellians of the Appennines. These statistics are from A. Schulten, Italische Namen und Stæmme, Beitræge zur alten Geschichte, II, 2, p. 171. The same proof comes from the likeness between the tombs here and in the Faliscan country: "Le tombe a casse soprapposte possono considerarsi come repositori per famiglie intere, e corrispondono alle grande tombe a loculo del territorio falisco". Not. d. Scavi, Ser. 5, 5 (1897), p. 257, from Mon. ant. pubb. dall'Acc. dei Lincei, Ant. falische, IV, p. 162.

[159]

Ed. Meyer, Geschichte des Altertums, V, p. 159.

[160]

Livy VI, 29; C.I.L., XIV, 2987.

[161]

Livy VII, 11; VII, 19; VIII, 12.

[162]

Præneste is not in the dedication list of Diana at Nemi, which dates about 500 B.C., Priscian, Cato IV, 4, 21 (Keil II, p. 129), and VII, 12, 60 (Keil II, p. 337). Livy II, 19, says Præneste deserted the Latins for Rome.

[163]

Livy VIII, 14.

[164]

Val. Max., De Superstitionibus, I, 3, 2; C.I.L., XIV, 2929, with Dessau's note.

[165]

See note 185.

[166]

"Præneste wird immer eine selbstændige Stellung eingenommen haben" Ed. Meyer, Geschichte des Alt., II, p. 523. Præneste is mentioned first of the league cities in the list given by [Aurelius Victor], Origo-gentis Rom., XVII, 6, and second in the list in Diodorus Siculus, VII, 5, 9 Vogel and also in Paulus, p. 159 (de Ponor). Præneste is called by Florus II, 9, 27 (III, 21, 27) one of the municipia Italiæ splendidissima along with Spoletium, Interamnium, Florentia.

[167]

Livy XXIII, 20, 2.

[168]

Livy I, 30, 1.

[169]

Cicero, de Leg., II, 2, 5.

[170]

Pauly-Wissowa, Real Enc. under "Anicia."

[171]

The old Oscan names in Pompeii, and the Etruscan names on the small grave stones of Cære, C.I.L., X, 3635-3692, are neither so numerous.

[172]

Dionysius III, 2.

[173]

Polybius VI, 14, 8; Livy XLIII, 2, 10.

[174]

Festus, p. 122 (de Ponor): Cives fuissent ut semper rempublicam separatim a populo Romano haberent, and supplemented, l.c., Pauli excerpta, p. 159 (de Ponor):

participes—fuerunt omnium rerum—præterquam de suffragio ferendo, aut magistratu capiendo.

[175]

Civitas sine suffragio, quorum civitas universa in civitatem Romanam venit, Livy VIII, 14; IX, 43; Festus, l.c., p. 159.

[176]

Paulus, p. 159 (de Ponor): Qui ad civitatem Romanam ita venerunt, ut municipes essent suæ cuiusque civitatis et coloniæ, ut Tiburtes, Prænestini, etc.

[177]

I do not think so. The argument is taken up later on page 73. It is enough to say here that Tusculum was estranged from the Latin League because she was made a municipium (Livy VI, 25-26), and how much less likely that Præneste would ever have taken such a status.

[178]

C. Gracchus in Gellius X, 3.

[179]

Tibur had censors in 204 B.C. (Livy XXIX, 15), and later again, C.I.L, I, 1113, 1120 = XIV, 3541, 3685. See also Marquardt, Staatsverwaltung, I, p. 159.

[180]

C.I.L, XIV, 171, 172, 2070.

[181]

C.I.L., XIV, 2169, 2213, 4195

[182]

Cicero, pro Milone, 10, 27; 17, 45; Asconius, in Milonianam, p. 27, l. 15 (Kiessling); C.I.L., XIV, 2097, 2110, 2112, 2121.

[183]

C.I.L., XIV, 3941, 3955.

[184]

Livy III, 18, 2; VI, 26, 4.

[185]

Livy IX, 16, 17; Dio, frag. 36, 24; Pliny XVII, 81. Ammianus Marcellinus XXX, 8, 5; compare Gellius X, 3, 2-4. This does not show, I think, what Dessau (C.I.L., XIV, p. 288) says it does: "quanta fuerit potestas imperatoris Romani in magistratus sociorum," but shows rather that the Roman dictator took advantage of his power to pay off some of the ancient grudge against the Latins, especially Præneste. The story of M. Marius at Teanum Sidicinum, and the provisions made at Cales and Ferentinum on that account, as told in Gellius X, 3, 2-3, also show plainly that not constitutional powers but arbitrary ones, are in question. In fact, it was in the year 173 B.C., that the consul L. Postumius Albinus, enraged at a previous cool reception at Præneste, imposed a burden on the magistrates of the town, which seems to have been held as an arbitrary political precedent. Livy XLII, 1: Ante hunc consulem NEMO umquam sociis in ULLA re oneri aut sumptui fuit.

[186]

Prænestinus prætor ... ex subsidiis suos duxerat, Livy IX, 16, 17.

[187]

A prætor led the contingent from Lavinium, Livy VIII, 11, 4; the prætor M. Anicius led from Præneste the cohort which gained such a reputation at Casilinum, Livy XXIII, 17-19. Strabo V, 249; cohors Pæligna, cuius præfectus, etc., proves nothing for a Latin contingent.

[188]

For the evidence that the consuls were first called prætors, see Pauly-Wissowa, Real Enc. under the word "consul" (Vol. IV, p. 1114) and the old Pauly under "prætor."

Mommsen, Staatsrecht, II, 1, p. 74, notes 1 and 2, from other evidence there quoted, and especially from Varro, de l.l., V, 80: prætor dictus qui præiret iure et exercitu, thinks that the consuls were not necessarily called prætors at first, but that probably even in the time of the kings the leader of the army was called the præ-itor. This is a modification of the statement six years earlier in Marquardt, Staatsverwaltung, I, p. 149, n. 4.

[189]

This caption I owe to Jos. H. Drake, Prof. of Roman Law at the University of Michigan.

[190]

Livy VIII, 3, 9; Dionysius III, 5, 3; 7, 3; 34, 3; V, 61.

[191]

Pauly-Wissowa under "dictator," and Mommsen, Staatsrecht, II, 171, 2.

[192]

Whether Egerius Lævius Tusculanus (Priscian, Inst., IV, p. 129 Keil) was dictator of the whole of the Latin league, as Beloch (Italischer Bund, p. 180) thinks, or not, according to Wissowa (Religion und Kultus der Roemer, p. 199), at least a dictator was the head of some sort of a Latin league, and gives us the name of the office (Pais, Storia di Roma, I, p. 335).

[193]

If it be objected that the survival of the dictatorship as a priestly office (Dictator Albanus, Orelli 2293, Marquardt, Staatsverw., I, p. 149, n. 2) means only a dictator for Alba Longa, rather than for the league of which Alba Longa seems to have been at one time the head, there can be no question about the Dictator Latina(rum) fer(iarum) caussa of the year 497 (C.I.L., I.p. 434 Fasti Cos. Capitolini), the same as in the year 208 B.C. (Livy XXVII, 33, 6). This survival is an exact parallel of the rex sacrorum in Rome (for references and discussion, see Marquardt, Staatsverw., III, p. 321), and the rex sacrificolus of Varro, de l.l. VI, 31. Compare Jordan, Topog. d. Stadt Rom, I, p. 508, n. 32, and Wissowa, Rel. u. Kult d. Roemer, p. 432. Note also that there were reges sacrorum in Lanuvium (C.I.L, XIV, 2089), Tusculum (C.I.L, XIV, 2634), Velitræ (C.I.L., X, 8417), Bovillæ (C.I.L., XIV, 2431 == VI, 2125). Compare also rex nemorensis, Suetonius, Caligula, 35 (Wissowa, Rel. u. Kult. d. Roemer, p. 199).

[194]

    C.I.L., XIV, 2990, 3000, 3001, 3002.

[195]

    C.I.L., XIV, 2890, 2902, 2906, 2994, 2999 (possibly 3008).

[196]

    C.I.L., XIV, 2975, 3000.

[197]

    C.I.L., XIV, 2990, 3001, 3002.

[198]

    See note 185 above.

[199]

    Livy XXIII, 17-19; Strabo V, 4, 10.

[200]

    Magistrates sociorum, Livy XLII, 1, 6-12.

[201]

    For references etc., see Beloch, Italischer Bund, p. 170, notes 1 and 2.

[202]

    The mention of one prætor in C.I.L., XIV, 2890, a dedication to Hercules, is later than other mention of two prætors, and is not irregular at any rate.

[203]

    C.I.L., XIV, 3000, two ædiles of the gens Saufeia, probably cousins. In C.I.L., XIV, 2890, 2902, 2906, 2975, 2990, 2994, 2999, 3000, 3001, 3002, 3008, out of eighteen prætors, ædiles, and quæstors mentioned, fifteen belong to the old families of Præneste, two to families that belong to the people living back in the Sabines, and one to a man from Fidenæ.

[204]

Cicero, pro Balbo, VIII, 21: Leges de civili iure sunt latæ: quas Latini voluerunt, adsciverunt; ipsa denique Iulia lege civitas ita est sociis et Latinis data ut, qui fundi populi facti non essent civitatem non haberent. Velleius Pater. II, 16: Recipiendo in civitatem, qui arma aut non ceperant aut deposuerant maturius, vires refectæ sunt. Gellius IV, 4, 3; Civitas universo Latio lege Iulia data est. Appian, Bell. Civ., I, 49: Ιταλιωτων δε τους ετι εν τη συμμαχια παραμενοντας εψηφισατο (η βουλη) ειναι πολιτας, ου δη μαλιστα μονον ου παντες επεθυμουν κτλ.

Marquardt, Staatsverw., I, p. 60; Greenidge, Roman Public Life, p. 311; Abbott, Roman Political Institutions, p. 102; Granrud, Roman Constitutional History, pp. 190-191.

[205]

Cicero, pro Archia, IV, 7: Data est civitas Silvani lege et Carbonis: si qui foederatis civitatibus adscripti fuissent, si tum cum lex ferebatur in Italia domicilium habuissent, et si sexaginta diebus apud prætorem essent professi. See also Schol. Bobiensia, p. 353 (Orelli corrects the mistake Silanus for Silvanus); Cicero, ad Fam., XIII, 30; Marquardt, Staatsverwaltung, I, p. 60. Greenidge, Roman Public Life, p. 311 thinks this law did not apply to any but the incolæ of federate communities; Abbott, Roman Political Institutions, p. 102.

[206]

Livy VIII, 14, 9: Tiburtes Prænestinique agro multati, neque ob recens tantum rebellionis commune cum aliis Latinis crimen, etc., ... ceterisque Latinis populis conubia commerciaque et concilia inter se ademerunt. Marquardt, Staatsverw., I, p. 46, n. 3, thinks not an æquum foedus, but from the words: ut is populus alterius populi maiestatem comiter conservaret, a clause in the treaty found in Proculus, Dig., 49, 15, 7 (Corpus Iuris Civ., I, p. 833) (compare Livy IX, 20, 8: sed ut in dicione populi Romani essent) thinks that the new treaty was an agreement based on dependence or clientage "ein Abhængigkeits—oder Clientelverhæltniss."

[207]

Mommsen, Geschichte des roem. Muenzwesens, p. 179 (French trans, de Blacas, I, p. 186), thinks two series of æs grave are to be assigned to Præneste and Tibur.

[208]

Livy XLIII, 2, 10: Furius Præneste, Matienus Tibur exulatum abierunt.

[209]

Polybius VI, 14, 8: εστι δ'ασφαλεια τοις φευγουσιν εν τε τη, Νεαπολιτω και Πραινεςτινων ετι δε Τιβουρινων πολει . Beloch, Italischer Bund, pp. 215, 221. Marquardt, Staatsverw., I, p. 45.

[210]

Livy XXIII, 20, 2; (Prænestini) civitate cum donarentur ob virtutem, non MUTAVERUNT.

[211]

The celebration of the feriæ Latinæ on Mons Albanus in 91 B.C., was to have been the scene of the spectacular beginning of the revolt against Rome, for the plan was to kill the two Roman consuls Iulius Cæsar and Marcius Philippus at that time. The presence of the Roman consuls and the attendance of the members of the old Latin league is proof of the outward continuance of the old foedus (Florus, II, 6 (III, 18)).

[212]

The lex Plautia-Papiria is the same as the law mentioned by Cicero, pro Archia, IV, 7, under the names of Silvanus and Carbo. The tribunes who proposed the law were C. Papirius Carbo and M. Plautius Silvanus. See Mommsen, Hermes 16 (1881), p. 30, n. 2. Also a good note in Long, Ciceronis Orationes, III, p. 215.

[213]

-

[213bis]

Appian, Bell. Civ., I, 65: εξεδραμεν ες τας αγχου πολεις, τας ου προ πολλου πολιτιδας Ρωμαιων μενομενας, Τιβυρτον τε και Πραινεστον, και οσαι μεχρι Νωλης. ερεθιζων απαντας ες αποστασιν, καιχρηματα ες τον πολεμον συλλεγων. See Dessau, C.I.L., XIV, p. 289.

It is worth noting that there is no thought of saying anything about Praaneste and Tibur, except to call them cities (πολεις). Had they been made municipia, after so many years of alliance as foederati, it seems likely that such a noteworthy change would have been specified.

Note also that for 88 B.C. Appian (Bell. Civ., I, 53) says: εως Ιταια πασα προσεχωρησει ες την Ρωμαιων πολιτειαν, χωρις γε Λευκανων καιΣαυνιτων τοτε.

[214]

Mommsen, Zum Roemischen Bodenrecht, Hermes 27 (1892), pp. 109 ff.

[215]

Marquardt, Staatsverw., I, p. 34.

[216]

Paulus, p. 159 (de Ponor): tertio, quum id genus hominum definitur, qui ad civitatem Romanam ita venerunt, ut municipes essent suæ cuiusque civitatis et coloniæ, ut Tiburtes, Prænestini, etc.

[217]

It is not strange perhaps, that there are no inscriptions which can be proved to date between 89 and 82 B.C., but inscriptions are numerous from the time of the empire, and although Tiberius granted Præneste the favor she asked, that of being a municipium, still no præfectus is found, not even a survival of the title.

The PRA ... in C.I.L., XIV, 2897, is præco, not præfectus, as I shall show soon in the publication of corrections of Præneste inscriptions, along with some new ones. For the government of a municipium, see Bull. dell'Inst., 1896, p. 7 ff.; Revue Arch., XXIX (1896), p. 398.

[218]

Mommsen, Hermes, 27 (1892), p. 109.

[219]

Marquardt, Staatsverw., I, p. 47 and note 3.

[220]

Val. Max. IX, 2, 1; Plutarch, Sulla, 32; Appian, Bell. Civ., I, 94; Lucan II, 194; Plutarch, præc. ger. reip., ch. 19 (p. 816); Augustinus, de civ. Dei, III, 28; Dessau, C.I.L., XIV, p. 289, n. 2.

[221]

One third of the land was the usual amount taken.

[222]

Note Mommsen's guess, as yet unproved (Hermes, 27 (1892), p. 109), that tribus, colonia, and duoviri iure dicundo go together, as do curia, municipium and IIIIviri i.d. and æd. pot.

[223]

Florus II, 9, 27 (III, 21): municipia Italiæ splendidissima sub hasta venierunt, Spoletium, Interamnium, Præneste, Florentia. See C.I.L., IX, 5074, 5075 for lack of distinction between colonia and municipium even in inscriptions. Florentia remained a colony (Mommsen, Hermes, 18 (1883), p. 176). Especially for difference in meaning of municipium from Roman and municipal point of view, see Marquardt, Staatsverw., I, p. 28, n. 2. For difference in earlier and later meaning of municipes, Marquardt, l.c., p. 34, n. 8. Valerius Maximus IX, 2, 1, speaking of Præneste in connection with Sulla says: quinque milia Prænestinorum extra moenia municipii evocata, where municipium means "town," and Dessau, C.I.L., XIV, p. 289, n. 1, speaking of the use of the word says: "ei rei non multum tribuerim."

[224]

Gellius XVI, 13, 5, ex colonia in municipii statum redegit. See Mommsen, Hermes, 18 (1883), p. 167.

[225]

Mommsen, Hermes, 27 (1892), p. 110; C.I.L., XIV, 2889: genio municipii; 2941, 3004: patrono municipii, which Dessau

[225 cont.]

(Hermes, 18 (1883), p. 167, n. 1) recognizes from the cutting as dating certainly later than Tiberius' time.

[226]

Regular colony officials appear all along in the incriptions down into the third century A.D.

[227]

Gellius XVI, 13, 5.

[228]

More in detail by Mommsen, Hermes, 27 (1892), p. 110.

[229]

Livy VII, 12, 8; VIII, 12, 8.

[230]

Mommsen, Hermes, 18 (1883), p. 161.

[231]

Cicero, pro P. Sulla, XXI, 61.

[232]

Niebuhr, R.G., II, 55, says the colonists from Rome were the patricians of the place, and were the only citizens who had full rights (civitas cum suffragio et iure honorum). Peter, Zeitschrift fuer Alterth., 1844, p. 198 takes the same view as Niebuhr. Against them are Kuhn, Zeitschrift fuer Alterth., 1854, Sec. 67-68, and Zumpt, Studia Rom., p. 367. Marquardt, Staatsverw., I, p. 36, n. 7, says that neither thesis is proved.

[233]

Dessau, C.I.L., XIV, p. 289.

[234]

Cicero, de leg. agr., II, 28, 78, complains that the property once owned by the colonists was now in the hands of a few. This means certainly, mostly bought up by old inhabitants, and a few does not mean a score, but few in comparison to the number of soldiers who had taken their small allotments of land.

[235]

C.I.L., XIV, p. 289.

[236]

C.I.L., XIV, 2964-2969.

[237]

-

[237bis]

C.I.L., XIV, 2964, 2965. No. 2964 dates before 14 A.D. when Augustus died, for had it been within the few years more which Drusus lived before he was poisoned by Sejanus in 23 A.D., he would have been termed divi Augusti nep. In the Acta Arvalium, C.I.L., VI, 2023a of 14 A.D. his name is followed by T i.f. and probably divi Augusti n.

[238]

C.I.L., XIV, 2966, 2968.

[239]

The first column of both inscriptions shows alternate lines spaced in, while the second column has the prænominal abbreviations exactly lined. More certain yet is the likeness which shows in a list of 27 names, and all but one without cognomina.

[240]

C.I.L., XIV, 2967.

[241]

Out of 201 examples of names from Præneste pigne inscriptions, in the C.I.L., XIV, in the Notizie degli Scavi of 1905 and 1907, in the unpublished pigne belonging both to the American School in Rome, and to the Johns Hopkins University, all but 15 are simple prænomina and nomina.

[242]

    C.I.L., X, 1233.

[243]

    C.I.L., IX, 422.

[244]

    Marquardt, Staatsverw., I, p. 161, n. 5.

[245]

    Lex Iulia Municipalis, C.I.L., I, 206, l. 142 ff. == Dessau, Inscrip. Lat. Sel., 6085.

[246]

    Marquardt, Staatsverw., I, p. 160.

[247]

    C.I.L., XIV, 2966.

[248]

    Pauly-Wissowa under "Dolabella," and "Cornelius," nos. 127-148.

[249]

    The real founder of Sulla's colony and the rebuilder of the city of Præneste seems to have been M. Terentius Varro Lucullus. This is argued by Vaglieri, who reports in Not. d. Scavi, 1907, p. 293 ff. the fragment of an architrave of some splendid building on which are the letters ... RO.LVCVL ... These letters Vaglieri thinks are cut in the style of the age of Sulla. They are fine deep letters, very well cut indeed, although they might perhaps be put a little later in date. An argument from the use of the name Terentia, as in the case of Cornelia, will be of some service here. The nomen Terentia was also very unpopular in Præneste. It occurs but seven times and every inscription is well down in the late imperial period. C.I.L., XIV, 3376, 3384, 2850, 4091, 75, 3273; Not. d. Scavi, 1896, p. 48.

[250]

C.I.L., XIV, 2967: ... elius Rufus Æd(ilis). I take him to be a Cornelius rather than an Ælius, because of the cognomen.

[251]

One Cornelius, a freedman (C.I.L., XIV, 3382), and three Corneliæ, freed women or slaves (C.I.L., XIV, 2992, 3032, 3361), but all at so late a date that the hatred or meaning of the name had been forgotten.

[252]

A full treatment of the use of the nomen Cornelia in Præneste will be published soon by the author in connection with his Prosographia Prænestina, and also something on the nomen Terentia (see note 92). The cutting of one of the two inscriptions under consideration, no. 2968, which fragment I saw in Præneste in 1907, bears out the early date. The larger fragment could not be seen.

[253]

Schulze, Zur Geschichte Lateinischer Eigennamen, p. 222, under "Rutenius." He finds the same form Rotanius only in Turin, Rutenius only in North Italy.

[254]

From the appearance of the name Rudia at Præneste (C.I.L., XIV, 3295) which Schulze (l.c., note 95) connects with Rutenia and Rotania, there is even a faint chance to believe that this Rotanius might have been a resident of Præneste before the colonization.

[255]

C.I.L., XIV, 3230-3237, 3315; Not. d. Scavi, 1905, p. 123; the one in question is C.I.L., XIV, 2966, I, 4.

[256]

C.I.L., VI, 22436: (Mess)iena Messieni, an inscription now in Warwick Castle, Warwick, England, supposedly from Rome, is the only instance of the name in the sepulcrales of the C.I.L., VI. In Præneste, C.I.L., XIV, 2966, I, 5, 3360; compare Schulze, Geschichte Lat. Eigennamen, p. 193, n. 6.

[257]

Cæsia at Præneste, C.I.L., XIV, 2852, 2966 I, 6, 2980, 3311, 3359, and the old form Ceisia, 4104.

[258]

See Schulze, l.c., index under Caleius.

[259]

C.I.L., XIV, 2964 II, 15.

[260]

Vibia especially in the old inscription C.I.L., XIV, 4098. Also in 2903, 2966 II, 9; Not. d. Scavi, 1900, p. 94.

[261]

Statioleia: C.I.L., XIV, 2966 I, 10, 3381.

[262]

C.I.L., XIV, 3210; Not. d. Scavi, 1905, p. 123; also found in two pigna inscriptions in the Johns Hopkins University collection, as yet unpublished.

[263]

There is a L. Aponius Mitheres on a basis in the Barberini garden in Præneste, but it may have come from Rome. The name is found Abonius in Etruria, but Aponia is found well scattered. See Schulze, Geschichte Lat. Eigennamen, p. 66.

[264]

C.I.L., XIV, 2855, 2626, 3336.

[265]

C.I.L., XIV, 3116. It may not be on a pigna.

[266]

Not. d. Scavi, 1907, p. 131. The nomen Paccia is a common name in the sepulchral inscriptions of Rome. C.I.L., VI, 23653-23675, but all are of a late date.

[267]

C.I.L., IX, 5016: C. Capive Vitali (Hadria).

[268]

A better restoration than Ninn(eius). The (N)inneius Sappæus (C.I.L., VI, 33610) is a freedman, and the inscription is late.

[269]

In the year 216 B.C. the Ninnii Celeres were hostages of Hannibal's at Capua (Livy XXIII, 8).

[270]

C.I.L., X, 2776-2779, but all late.

[271]

C.I.L., X, 885-886. A Ninnius was procurator to Domitian, according to a fistula plumbea found at Rome (Bull. Com., 1882, p. 171, n. 597). A.Q. Ninnius Hasta was consul ordinarius in 114 A.D. (C.I.L., XI, 3614, compare Paulus, Dig. 48, 8, 5 [Corpus Iuris Civ., I, p. 802]). See also a Ninnius Crassus, Dessau, Prosographia Imp. Romani, II, p. 407, n. 79.

[272]

It is interesting to note that C. Paccius and C. Ninnius are officials, one would guess duovirs, of the same year in Pompeii, and thus parallel the men here in Præneste: C.I.L., X, 885-886: N. Paccius Chilo and M. Ninnius Pollio, who in 14 B.C. are duoviri v.a.s.p.p. (viis annonæ sacris publicis procurandis), Henzen; (votis Augustalibus sacris publicis procurandis), Mommsen; (viis ædibus, etc.), Cagnat; See Liebenam in Pauly-Wissowa, Real Encyc., V, 1842, 9.

[273]

Liebenam in Pauly-Wissowa, Real Encyc., V, 1806.

[274]

Marquardt, Staatsverw., I, p. 157 ff.; Liebenam in Pauly-Wissowa, Real Enc., V, 1825. Sometimes the officers were designated simply quinquennales, and this seems to have been the early method. For all the various differences in the title, see Marquardt, l.c., p. 160, n. 13.

[275]

All at least except the regimen morum, so Marquardt, l.c., p. 162 and n. 2.

[276]

Marquardt, Staatsverw., I, p. 161, n. 6.

[277]

Marquardt, Staatsverw., I, p. 161, n. 7.

[278]

Beloch, Italischer Bund, p. 78 ff.; Nissen, Italische Landeskunde, II, p. 99 ff.

[279]

C.I.L., IX, 422 = Dessau, Insc. Lat. Sel., 6123.

[280]

C.I.L., X, 1233 = Dessau 6124.

[281]

Near Aquinum. C.I.L., X, 5405 = Dessau 6125.

[282]

C.I.L., XIV, 245 = Dessau 6126.

[283]

C.I.L., XIV, 2964.

[284]

He is not even mentioned in Pauly-Wissowa or Ruggiero.

[285]

C.I.L., XIV, 2966.

[286]

    C.I.L., XIV, 2964.

[287]

    C.I.L., XIV, 2965.

[288]

    Marquardt, Staatsverw., I, p. 169 for full discussion, with references to other cases.

[289]

    C.I.L., XIV, 172: præt(or) Laur(entium) Lavin(atium) IIIIvir q(uin) q(uennalis) Fæsulis.

[290]

    C.I.L., XIV, 3599.

[291]

    C.I.L., XIV, 3609.

[292]

    C.I.L., XIV, 3650.

[293]

    C.I.L., I, 1236 == X, 1573 == Dessau 6345.

[294]

    C.I.L., XIV, 3665.

[295]

    C.I.L., XI, 421 == Dessau 6662.

[296]

    C. Alfius C.f. Lem. Ruf(us) IIvir quin(q). col. Iul. Hispelli et IIvir quinq. in municipio suo Casini, C.I.L., XI, 5278 == Dessau 6624. Bormann, C.I.L., XI, p. 766, considers this to be an inscription of the time of Augustus and thinks the man here mentioned is one of his colonists.

[297]

    Not. d. Scav, 1884, p. 418 == Dessau 6598.

[298]

    C.I.L., IX, 5831 == Dessau 6572.

[299]

    C.I.L., IX, 3311 == Dessau 6532.

[300]

    L. Septimio L.f. Arn. Calvo. æd., IIIIvir. i.d., præf. ex s.c. [q]uinquennalicia potestate, etc., Eph. Ep. 8, 120 == Dessau 6527.

[301]

    C.I.L., IX, 1618 == Dessau 6507.

[302]

    C.I.L., IX, 652 == Dessau 6481.

[303]

    The full title is worth notice: IIIIvir i(ure) d(icundo) q(uinquennalis) c(ensoria) p(otestate), C.I.L., X, 49 == Dessau 6463.

[304]

    C.I.L., X, 344 == Dessau 6450.

[305]

    C.I.L., X, 1036 == Dessau 6365.

[306]

    C.I.L., X, 840 == Dessau 6362: M. Holconio Celeri d.v.i.d. quinq. designato. Augusti sacerdoti.

[307]

    C.I.L., X, 1273 == Dessau 6344.

[308]

C.I.L., X, 4641 == Dessau 6301.

[309]

C.I.L., X, 5401 == Dessau 6291.

[310]

C.I.L., X, 5393 == Dessau 6286.

[311]

C.I.L., XIV, 4148.

[312]

C.I.L., XIV, 4097, 4105a, 4106f.

[313]

C.I.L., XIV, 2795.

[314]

C.I.L., XIV, 4237. Another case of the same kind is seen in the fragment C.I.L., XIV, 4247.

[315]

Zangemeister, C.I.L., IV., Index, shows 75 duoviri and but 4 quinquennales.

[316]

L. Veranius Hypsæus 6 times: C.I.L., IV, 170, 187, 193, 200, 270, 394(?). Q. Postumius Modestus 7 times: 195, 279, 736, 756, 786, 1156. Only two other men appear, one 3 times; 214, 596, 824, the other once: 504.

[317]

(1) Verulæ, C.I.L., X, 5796; Acerræ, C.I.L., X, 3759; (2) Anagnia, C.I.L., X, 5919; Allifæ, C.I.L., IX, 2354; Æclanum, C.I.L., IX, 1160; (3) Sutrium, C.I.L., XI, 3261; Tergeste, C.I.L., V, 545; (4) Tibur, C.I.L., XIV, 3665; Ausculum Apulorum, C.I.L., IX, 668; Sora, C.I.L, X, 5714; (5) Formiæ, C.I.L., X, 6101; Pompeii, C.I.L., X, 1036; (6) Ferentinum, C.I.L., X, 5844, 5853; Falerii,

C.I.L., XI, 3123; (7) Pompeii, Not. d. Scavi, 1898, p. 171, and C.I.L., X, 788, 789, 851; Bovianum, C.I.L., IX, 2568; (8) Telesia, C.I.L., IX, 2234; Allifæ, C.I.L., IX, 2353; Hispellum, C.I.L., XI, 5283.

[318]

The same certainly as M. Antonius Sobarus of 4091,17 and duovir with T. Diadumenius, as is shown by the connective et. Compare 4091, 4, 6, 7.

[319]

C.I.L., I, p. 311 reads Lucius, which is certainly wrong. There is but one Lucius in Dessau, Prosographia Imp. Rom.; there is however a Lucilius with this same cognomen Dessau, l.c.

[320]

Probably not the M. Iuventius Laterensis, the Roman quæstor, for the brick stamps of Præneste in other cases seem to show the quæstors of the city.